AmblesideOnline Poetry Anthology

Volume Four

Alfred, Lord Tennyson
Emily Dickinson
William Wordsworth

Edited and annotated by the AmblesideOnline Educational Foundation

AmblesideOnline Poetry Anthology, Volume Four: Alfred, Lord Tennyson, Emily Dickinson, William Wordsworth

Copyright © 2021 by AmblesideOnline Educational Foundation

Cover design by Bryan White

ISBN: 9798450053721

Table of Contents

Introduction to the Series

Charlotte Mason said that poetry is an instructor of the conscience, and that children "must grow up upon the best… There is never a time when they are unequal to worthy thoughts, well put; inspiring tales, well told. Let Blake's 'Songs of Innocence' represent their standard in poetry…" and the result will be readers who demand the best, "the fit and beautiful expression of inspiring ideas and pictures of life" (*Parents and Children*, p. 263).

And modern research supports her claim. Researchers at the University of Liverpool found that reading poetry provides a "rocket-boost" to the brain that cannot be matched by straightforward, simple paraphrases. The research also found that poetry, in particular, "increased activity in the right hemisphere of the brain, an area concerned with 'autobiographical memory,' which helped the reader to reflect on and reappraise their own experiences in light of what they had read" (*Daily Mail*, Jan. 13, 2013).

AmblesideOnline students read a variety of poems which offer them word pictures and ideas to reflect on, and to help them interpret their own experiences.

> "[A student] should have practice, too, in reading aloud, for the most part, in the books he is using for his term's work. These should include a good deal of poetry, to accustom him to the delicate rendering of shades of meaning, and especially to make him aware that words are beautiful in themselves, that they are a source of pleasure, and are worthy of our honour; and that a beautiful word deserves to be beautifully said, with a certain roundness of tone and precision of utterance. Quite young children are open to this sort of teaching, conveyed, not in a lesson, but by a word now and then." (Charlotte Mason, *Home Education*, p. 227)

Please don't analyze and dissect these poems. There is time for that later in your young scholar's life. Just as there is a time to simply feed your young ones delicious, nourishing food, and a time later in their lives to teach them the analytical details of health, nutrition, and all about the vitamins and minerals in their food, there is a time to just read poetry and learn to enjoy it. "The thing is," Charlotte Mason said in a book she wrote for children, "to keep your eye upon words and wait to feel their force and beauty; and, when words are so fit that no other words can be put in their places, so few that none can be left out without spoiling the sense, and so fresh and musical that they delight you, then you may be sure that you are reading Literature, whether in prose or poetry. A great deal of delightful literature can be recognised only by this test." (*Ourselves Book I*, p. 41)

We hope you will enjoy reading these poems together as much as we enjoy sharing them with you.

An added note: we have tried to be sensitive to the changing language and ideas of our present day, while presenting these poems from the past as faithfully as we were able. However, it is beyond our capabilities to anticipate every new word meaning that exists or that arises in the future. We can only give the same advice and disclaimer that we would suggest for other studies, from literature through science: please preview this material, and then use it with care and discretion.

Donna-Jean Breckenridge
Lynn Bruce
Wendi Capehart
Karen Glass
Leslie Laurio
Anne White

Foreword to Volume Four

by Donna-Jean Breckenridge

We sat in a courtyard in the Florida sunshine. The sky was a brilliant blue above us, the breeze moved the fronds of the tall Royal Palm nearby. It was warm, very warm, to my northern sensibilities, but my grandmother was enveloped in an afghan and a few layers of sweaters. She sat quietly in the wheelchair, and we sat with her. Ninety-nine years is a long time to live, but now it seemed she had forgotten nearly all of it. She had maybe even forgotten us.

In the quiet, a flood of memories washed over me. My Mimi, from England's Lake District, who made every summer fun, every Christmas special, every sitting-next-to-her-in-church important, now did not speak, did not respond. It was enough, though, just to hold her hand.

I thought of her years of reading through the Bible, cover to cover ("Sixty times," she once told my Dad, and I know there were many more after that). And I remembered how often I would see her curled up on the couch, poetry book in hand. She read poetry to me, recited poetry with me, and bought me books of poetry—Dickinson, Longfellow, Burns, and always, always Wordsworth ("My countryman!" she would brag about him).

And in the final years, when our visits were few but our phone calls continued until her world went quiet, she asked me how our little homeschool was going, and what we were learning. She was so delighted to hear that we read poetry together.

In the stillness of that Florida morning, my Mom read to her from the book of Psalms and some from Philippians, and we saw the familiar light reappear in her tired blue eyes. There was a nearly imperceptible nod, and I knew she was hearing the words she knew so well, the words that gave her strength. And as I read aloud a few lines from "Ode: Intimations of Immortality," I saw her lips move, ever so gently, as she formed the words of that beloved poem. Across some barrier we did not understand, we shared deep truths and touched one another's spirits. She had not forgotten.

When she died a few months later, there had indeed "past away a glory from the earth." At her service, we read the Scriptures and some of her favorite poems (yes, Wordsworth). Ever since then, every day when I sit with my children—and now my grandchildren—I think of her as I read our poems. I can still hear the lilt of her accent as she would quote for me,

> "The angel paused in his downward flight
> With seeds of love and truth and light;
> And said, 'Oh, where shall this seed be sown,
> That it yield most fruit when fully grown?'
> The Savior paused and said as He smiled,
> 'Place it for me in the heart of a child.'"

> (From the book *Bread from My Oven*, by Marjorie Parker)

Alfred, Lord Tennyson (1809-1892)

Biographical Sketch by Donna-Jean Breckenridge

"I hold it true,
Whate'er befall;
'Tis better to have loved and lost
Than never to have loved at all."

These oft-quoted lines by the man known as Alfred, Lord Tennyson, come from his lengthy poem, "In Memoriam." And while the typical assumption is that the poem was written after the deep pain of a broken romance, the added initials in the title, "A.H.H.," tell the full story. "A.H.H." stands for Arthur Henry Hallam, Tennyson's dear friend who died suddenly at the age of 22. Hallam, a brilliant fellow poet and classmate at Trinity College at Cambridge, had been engaged to marry Tennyson's sister, Emily.

"In Memoriam" was considered one of the greatest poems of the nineteenth century. It was loved by Queen Victoria herself, who told Tennyson that after the death of her husband, Prince Albert, she was "soothed and pleased by it."

In his day, Tennyson was said to be one of the three most famous living persons. He shared that fame with none other than Queen Victoria and British politician and Prime Minister William Gladstone. Tennyson was also England's Poet Laureate, succeeding William Wordsworth.

Alfred Tennyson (the "Lord" came when he accepted a peerage from the Queen while he was in his seventies) was born in 1809, one of his parents' eleven surviving children. His father, a minister, suffered by his own father's neglect and disinheritance, and he took it out on his family. Alfred's father provided an atmosphere of books and learning, yet he was an alcoholic who struggled mentally and physically.

Tennyson's years in college were his happiest. He was able to leave home, his first book of poetry was published, and he had his friendship with Hallam and other young poets. But the older Tennyson died, and Alfred was unable to finish his education. His second book of poems received – at least initially – poor reviews, his relationship with a young woman ended because of his inadequate finances, and then there was the tragedy of Hallam's sudden death.

For ten years, Tennyson published no more poems. He did continue to write, however, and in 1850, things began to improve. He learned he did not have an illness that had gripped him with fear, his financial situation stabilized, he was married to Emily Sellwood, he published "In Memoriam" to much acclaim (it was his wife who suggested the title), and he was selected to be England's new Poet Laureate.

Tennyson's fame came at the cost of privacy. People would look through the windows of his home while he and his family ate their meals, and they soon had to move. Tennyson went on to write more poetry, including "Charge of the Light Brigade" and the twelve narrative poems that make up the Arthurian epic "Idylls of the King."

Despite his success, he continued to experience tragedy. One of his sons, Lionel, got sick and died while traveling back from a trip to India. Tennyson's "Demeter and Other Poems" includes some poetry that addressed this great loss.

In 1892, at the age of 83, Tennyson died at his home. A week later, he was buried in Westminster Abbey's Poets' Corner.

Tennyson, particularly in his later years, spent much time in grief, searching for proofs of immortality. Yet he asked that every edition of his poetry end with the simple prayer found in his poem, "Crossing the Bar":

> Sunset and evening star,
> And one clear call for me!
> And may there be no moaning of the bar,
> When I put out to sea,
> But such a tide as moving seems asleep,
> Too full for sound or foam,
> When that which drew from out the boundless deep
> Turns again home.
> Twilight and evening bell,
> And after that the dark!
> And may there be no sadness of farewell;

When I embark;
For tho' from out our bourne of Time and Place
The flood may bear me far,
I hope to see my pilot face to face
When I have crossed the bar.

---

01. Cradle Song

What does little birdie say
In her nest at peep of day?
Let me fly, says little birdie,
Mother, let me fly away.

Birdie, rest a little longer,
Till the little wings are stronger,
So she rests a little longer,
Then she flies away.

What does little baby say,
In her bed at peep of day?
Baby says, like little birdie,
Let me rise and fly away.

Baby, sleep a little longer,
Till the little limbs are stronger,
If she sleeps a little longer,
Baby too shall fly away.

02. The Eagle

He clasps the crag with crooked hands;
Close to the sun in lonely lands,
Ring'd with the azure world, he stands.

The wrinkled sea beneath him crawls;
He watches from his mountain walls,
And like a thunderbolt he falls.

03. Strong Son of God, Immortal Love

Strong Son of God, immortal Love,
Whom we, that have not seen thy face,
By faith, and faith alone, embrace,
Believing where we cannot prove;

Thine are these orbs of light and shade;
Thou madest Life in man and brute;
Thou madest Death; and lo, thy foot
Is on the skull which thou hast made.

Thou wilt not leave us in the dust:
Thou madest man, he knows not why,
He thinks he was not made to die;
And thou hast made him: thou art just.

Thou seemest human and divine,
The highest, holiest manhood, thou:
Our wills are ours, we know not how;
Our wills are ours, to make them thine.

Our little systems have their day;
They have their day and cease to be:

They are but broken lights of thee,
And thou, O Lord, art more than they.

We have but faith: we cannot know;
For knowledge is of things we see;
And yet we trust it comes from thee,
A beam in darkness: let it grow.

Let knowledge grow from more to more,
But more of reverence in us dwell;
That mind and soul, according well,
May make one music as before,

But vaster. We are fools and slight;
We mock thee when we do not fear:
But help thy foolish ones to bear;
Help thy vain worlds to bear thy light.

Forgive what seem'd my sin in me;
What seem'd my worth since I began;
For merit lives from man to man,
And not from man, O Lord, to thee.

Forgive my grief for one removed,
Thy creature, whom I found so fair.
I trust he lives in thee, and there
I find him worthier to be loved.

Forgive these wild and wandering cries,
Confusions of a wasted youth;
Forgive them where they fail in truth,
And in thy wisdom make me wise.

04. Ring Out, Wild Bells

Ring out, wild bells, to the wild sky,
The flying cloud, the frosty light;
The year is dying in the night;
Ring out, wild bells, and let him die.

Ring out the old, ring in the new,
Ring, happy bells, across the snow;
The year is going, let him go;
Ring out the false, ring in the true.

Ring out the grief that saps the mind,
For those that here we see no more,
Ring out the feud of rich and poor,
Ring in redress to all mankind.

Ring out a slowly dying cause,
And ancient forms of party strife;
Ring in the nobler modes of life,
With sweeter manners, purer laws.

Ring out the want, the care, the sin,
The faithless coldness of the times;
Ring out, ring out my mournful rhymes,
But ring the fuller minstrel in.

Ring out false pride in place and blood,
The civic slander and the spite;
Ring in the love of truth and right,
Ring in the common love of good.

Ring out old shapes of foul disease,
Ring out the narrowing lust of gold;
Ring out the thousand wars of old,
Ring in the thousand years of peace.

Ring in the valiant man and free,
The larger heart, the kindlier hand;
Ring out the darkness of the land,
Ring in the Christ that is to be.

05. The Kraken

Below the thunders of the upper deep;
Far, far beneath in the abysmal sea,
His ancient, dreamless, uninvaded sleep
The Kraken sleepeth: faintest sunlights flee
About his shadowy sides: above him swell
Huge sponges of millennial growth and height;
And far away into the sickly light,
From many a wondrous grot and secret cell
Unnumber'd and enormous polypi
Winnow with giant arms the slumbering green.
There hath he lain for ages and will lie
Battening upon huge seaworms in his sleep,
Until the latter fire shall heat the deep;
Then once by man and angels to be seen,
In roaring he shall rise and on the surface die.

06. The Sea-Fairies

Slow sail'd the weary mariners and saw,
Betwixt the green brink and the running foam,
Sweet faces, rounded arms, and bosoms prest
To little harps of gold; and while they mused,
Whispering to each other half in fear,
Shrill music reach'd them on the middle sea.

Whither away, whither away, whither away? fly no more.
Whither away, from the high green field, and the happy
blossoming shore?
Day and night to the billow the fountain calls;
Down shower the gambolling waterfalls
From wandering over the lea;
Out of the live-green heart of the dells
They freshen the silvery-crimson shells,
And thick with white bells the clover-hill swells
High over the full-toned sea.
O, hither, come hither and furl your sails,
Come hither to me and to me;
Hither, come hither and frolic and play;
Here it is only the mew that wails;
We will sing to you all the day.
Mariner, mariner, furl your sails,
For here are the blissful downs and dales,
And merrily, merrily carol the gales,
And the spangle dances in bight and bay,
And the rainbow forms and flies on the land
Over the islands free;
And the rainbow lives in the curve of the sand;
Hither, come hither and see;
And the rainbow hangs on the poising wave,

And sweet is the color of cove and cave,
And sweet shall your welcome be.
O, hither, come hither, and be our lords,
For merry brides are we.
We will kiss sweet kisses, and speak sweet words;
O, listen, listen, your eyes shall glisten
With pleasure and love and jubilee.
O, listen, listen, your eyes shall glisten
When the sharp clear twang of the golden chords
Runs up the ridged sea.
Who can light on as happy a shore
All the world o'er, all the world o'er?
Whither away? listen and stay; mariner, mariner,
fly no more.

07. Break, Break, Break

Break, break, break,
On thy cold gray stones, O Sea!
And I would that my tongue could utter
The thoughts that arise in me.

O, well for the fisherman's boy,
That he shouts with his sister at play!
O, well for the sailor lad,
That he sings in his boat on the bay!

And the stately ships go on
To their haven under the hill;
But O for the touch of a vanish'd hand,
And the sound of a voice that is still!

Break, break, break,
At the foot of thy crags, O Sea!
But the tender grace of a day that is dead
Will never come back to me.

08. Charge of the Light Brigade

The Charge of the Light Brigade took place at the Battle of Balaclava, during the Crimean War, in October 1854. The Light Brigade was a British cavalry unit that expected to be sent to prevent Russian forces from removing captured Turkish guns. Due to miscommunication and other errors, they were sent to attack a different Russian unit, one which immediately shot back at them. The Light Brigade was not destroyed, but many of the men were killed, wounded, or taken prisoner. Tennyson's poem about the courage of these soldiers was published just six weeks after the event.

 Some collections include a version of The Light Brigade with modernized punctuation. We have chosen to print it as it first appeared in Tennyson's Poems.

Half a league, half a league,
Half a league onward,
All in the valley of Death
 Rode the six hundred.
"Forward, the Light Brigade!
Charge for the guns!" he said:
Into the valley of Death
 Rode the six hundred.

"Forward, the Light Brigade!"
Was there a man dismay'd?
Not tho' the soldier knew
 Some one had blunder'd:
Their's not to make reply,
Their's not to reason why,
Their's but to do and die:

Into the valley of Death
    Rode the six hundred.

Cannon to right of them,
Cannon to left of them,
Cannon in front of them
    Volley'd and thunder'd;
Storm'd at with shot and shell,
Boldly they rode and well,
Into the jaws of Death,
Into the mouth of Hell
    Rode the six hundred.

Flash'd all their sabres bare,
Flash'd as they turn'd in air
Sab'ring the gunners there,
Charging an army, while
    All the world wonder'd:
Plunged in the battery-smoke,
Right thro' the line they broke;
Cossack and Russian
Reel'd from the sabre-stroke
    Shatter'd and sunder'd.
Then they rode back, but not —
    Not the six hundred.

Cannon to right of them,
Cannon to left of them,
Cannon behind them
    Volley'd and thunder'd;
Storm'd at with shot and shell,
While horse and hero fell,
They that had fought so well

Came thro' the jaws of Death,
Back from the mouth of Hell,
All that was left of them,
    Left of six hundred.

When can their glory fade?
O the wild charge they made!
    All the world wonder'd.
Honour the charge they made!
Honour the Light Brigade,
    Noble six hundred!

09. The Oak

Live thy life,
    Young and old,
Like yon oak,
Bright in spring,
    Living gold;

Summer-rich
    Then; and then
Autumn-changed,
Soberer hued
    Gold again.

All his leaves
    Fall'n at length,
Look, he stands,
Trunk and bough,
    Naked strength.

10. In Memoriam, VII

Dark house, by which once more I stand
Here in the long unlovely street,
Doors, where my heart was used to beat
So quickly, waiting for a hand,

A hand that can be clasped no more —
Behold me, for I cannot sleep,
And like a guilty thing I creep
At earliest morning to the door.

He is not here; but far away
The noise of life begins again
And ghastly through the drizzling rain
On the bald street breaks the blank day.

11. The Splendor Falls

from *The Princess*

The splendor falls on castle walls
And snowy summits old in story:
The long light shakes across the lakes
And the wild cataract leaps in glory.
Blow, bugle, blow, set the wild echoes flying,
Blow, bugle; answer, echoes—dying, dying, dying.

O hark, O hear! how thin and clear,
And thinner, clearer, farther going!
O sweet and far from cliff and scar
The horns of Elfland faintly blowing!
Blow, let us hear the purple glens replying,
Blow, bugle; answer, echoes—dying, dying, dying.

O love they die in yon rich sky,
They faint on hill or field, or river:
Our echoes roll from soul to soul,
And grow forever and forever.
Blow, bugle, blow, set the wild echoes flying,
And answer, echoes, answer—dying, dying, dying.

12. Tears, Idle Tears

from *The Princess*

Tears, idle tears, I know not what they mean,
Tears from the depth of some divine despair
Rise in the heart, and gather to the eyes,
In looking on the happy Autumn-fields,
And thinking of the days that are no more.

Fresh as the first beam glittering on a sail,
That brings our friends up from the underworld,
Sad as the last which reddens over one
That sinks with all we love below the verge;
So sad, so fresh, the days that are no more.

Ah, sad and strange as in dark summer dawns
The earliest pipe of half-awakened birds
To dying ears, when unto dying eyes
The casement slowly grows a glimmering square;
So sad, so strange, the days that are no more.

Dear as remembered kisses after death,
And sweet as those by hopeless fancy feigned
On lips that are for others; deep as love,

Deep as first love, and wild with all regret;
O Death in Life, the days that are no more!

13. from The Palace of Art

I built my soul a lordly pleasure-house,
    Wherein at ease for aye to dwell.
I said, "O Soul, make merry and carouse,
    Dear soul, for all is well."

A huge crag-platform, smooth as burnish'd brass,
    I chose. The ranged ramparts bright
From level meadow-bases of deep grass
    Suddenly scaled the light.

Thereon I built it firm. Of ledge or shelf
    The rock rose clear, or winding stair.
My soul would live alone unto herself
    In her high palace there.

To which my soul made answer readily:
    "Trust me, in bliss I shall abide
In this great mansion, that is built for me,
    So royal-rich and wide."

Full of long-sounding corridors it was,
    over-vaulted grateful gloom,
Thro' which the livelong day my soul did pass,
    Well-pleased, from room to room.

14. Sweet and Low

from *The Princess*

Sweet and low, sweet and low,
Wind of the western sea,
Low, low, breathe and blow,
Wind of the western sea!
Over the rolling waters go,
Come from the dying moon, and blow,
Blow him again to me;
While my little one, while my pretty one, sleeps.

Sleep and rest, sleep and rest,
Father will come to thee soon;
Rest, rest, on mother's breast,
Father will come to thee soon;
Father will come to his babe in the nest,
Silver sails all out of the west
Under the silver moon;
Sleep, my little one, sleep, my pretty one, sleep.

15. Ask Me No More

from *The Princess*

Ask me no more: the moon may draw the sea;
    The cloud may stoop from heaven and take the shape,
    With fold to fold, of mountain or of cape;
But O too fond, when have I answer'd thee?
        Ask me no more.

Ask me no more: what answer should I give?
    I love not hollow cheek or faded eye:

Yet, O my friend, I will not have thee die!
Ask me no more, lest I should bid thee live;
     Ask me no more.

Ask me no more: thy fate and mine are seal'd:
     I strove against the stream and all in vain:
     Let the great river take me to the main:
No more, dear love, for at a touch I yield;
     Ask me no more.

16. The Flower

Once in a golden hour
     I cast to earth a seed.
Up there came a flower,
     The people said, a weed.

To and fro they went
     Thro' my garden bower,
And muttering discontent
     Cursed me and my flower.

Then it grew so tall
     It wore a crown of light,
But thieves from o'er the wall
     Stole the seed by night.

Sow'd it far and wide
     By every town and tower,
Till all the people cried,
     "Splendid is the flower!"

Read my little fable:
    He that runs may read.
Most can raise the flowers now,
    For all have got the seed.

And some are pretty enough,
    And some are poor indeed;
And now again the people
    Call it but a weed.

17. A Farewell

Flow down, cold rivulet, to the sea,
    Thy tribute wave deliver;
No more by thee my steps shall be,
    For ever and for ever.

Flow, softly flow, by lawn and lea,
    A rivulet then a river;
Nowhere by thee my steps shall be,
    For ever and for ever.

But here will sigh thine alder tree;
    And here thine aspen shiver;
And here by thee will hum the bee,
    For ever and for ever.

A thousand suns will stream on thee,
    A thousand moons will quiver;
But not by thee my steps shall be,
    For ever and for ever.

18. Of Old Sat Freedom

Of old sat Freedom on the heights,
The thunders breaking at her feet;
Above her shook the starry lights;
She heard the torrents meet.

There in her place she did rejoice,
Self-gather'd in her prophet-mind,
But fragments of her mighty voice
Came rolling on the wind.

Then stept she down thro' town and field
To mingle with the human race,
And part by part to men reveal'd
The fullness of her face –

Grave mother of majestic works,
From her isle-alter gazing down,
Who, God-like, grasps the triple forks,
And, king-like, wears the crown:
Her open eyes desire the truth.
The wisdom of a thousand years
Is in them. May perpetual youth
Keep dry their light from tears;

That her fair form may stand and shine,
Make bright our days and light our dreams,
Turning to scorn with lips divine
The falsehood of extremes!

19. The Blackbird

A jenneting is a type of apple that ripens early in the growing season. Espaliers are fruit trees or shrubs trained to grow against a wall or lattice.

O blackbird! sing me something well:
    While all the neighbors shoot thee round,
    I keep smooth plats of fruitful ground,
Where thou mayst warble, eat, and dwell.

The espaliers and the standards all
    Are thine; the range of lawn and park;
    The unnetted black-hearts ripen dark,
All thine, against the garden wall.

Yet, tho' I spared thee all the spring,
    Thy sole delight is, sitting still,
    With that gold dagger of thy bill
To fret the summer jenneting.

A golden bill! the silver tongue,
    Cold February loved, is dry;
    Plenty corrupts the melody
That made thee famous once, when young:

And in the sultry garden-squares,
    Now thy flute-notes are changed to coarse,
    I hear thee not at all, or hoarse
As when a hawker hawks his wares.
Take warning! he that will not sing
    While yon sun prospers in the blue,
    Shall sing for want, ere leaves are new,
Caught in the frozen palms of Spring.

20. Circumstance

Two children in two neighbor villages
Playing mad pranks along the heathy leas;
Two strangers meeting at a festival;
Two lovers whispering by an orchard wall;
Two lives bound fast in one with golden ease;
Two graves grass-green beside a gray church-tower,
Wash'd with still rains and daisy-blossomed;
Two children in one hamlet born and bred;
So runs the round of life from hour to hour.

21. The Death of the Old Year

Full knee-deep lies the winter snow,
And the winter winds are wearily sighing;
Toll ye the church-bell sad and slow,
And tread softly and speak low,
For the old year lies a-dying.
    Old year, you must not die;
    You came to us so readily,
    You lived with us so steadily,
    Old year, you shall not die.

He lieth still, he doth not move,
He will not see the dawn of day.
He hath no other life above.
He gave me a friend, and a true true-love,
And the New-year will take 'em away.
    Old year, you must not go;
    So long as you have been with us,
    Such joy as you have seen with us,
    Old year, you shall not go.

He froth'd his bumpers to the brim;
A jollier year we shall not see.
But tho' his eyes are waxing dim,
And tho' his foes speak ill of him,
He was a friend to me.
    Old year, you shall not die;
      We did so laugh and cry with you,
      I've half a mind to die with you,
    Old year, if you must die.

He was full of joke and jest,
But all his merry quips are o'er.
To see him die, across the waste
His son and heir doth ride post-haste,
But he'll be dead before.
    Every one for his own.
      The night is starry and cold, my friend,
      And the New-year blithe and bold, my friend,
    Comes up to take his own.

How hard he breathes! over the snow
I heard just now the crowing cock.
The shadows flicker to and fro;
The cricket chirps; the light burns low;
'Tis nearly twelve o'clock.
    Shake hands, before you die.
      Old year, we'll dearly rue for you.
      What is it we can do for you?
    Speak out before you die.

His face is growing sharp and thin.
Alack! our friend is gone.
Close up his eyes; tie up his chin;

Step from the corpse, and let him in
That standeth there alone,
    And waiteth at the door.
    There's a new foot on the floor, my friend,
    And a new face at the door, my friend,
    A new face at the door.

22. The Deserted House

Life and Thought have gone away
    Side by side,
    Leaving door and windows wide;
Careless tenants they!
All within is dark as night:
In the windows is no light;
And no murmur at the door,
So frequent on its hinge before.

Close the door, the shutters close,
    Or thro' the windows we shall see
    The nakedness and vacancy
Of the dark deserted house.

Come away; no more of mirth
    Is here or merry-making sound.
The house was builded of the earth,
    And shall fall again to ground.

Come away; for Life and Thought
    Here no longer dwell,
      But in a city glorious —
A great and distant city —have bought

A mansion incorruptible.
Would they could have stayed with us!

23. The Dying Swan

Coronach is a funeral song; shawm is a woodwind instrument.

The plain was grassy, wild and bare,
Wide, wild, and open to the air,
Which had built up everywhere
An under-roof of doleful gray.
With an inner voice the river ran,
Adown it floated a dying swan,
And loudly did lament.
It was the middle of the day.
Ever the weary wind went on,
And took the reed-tops as it went.

Some blue peaks in the distance rose,
And white against the cold-white sky,
Shone out their crowning snows.
One willow over the river wept,
And shook the wave as the wind did sigh;
Above in the wind was the swallow,
Chasing itself at its own wild will,
And far thro' the marish green and still
The tangled water-courses slept,
Shot over with purple, and green, and yellow.

The wild swan's death-hymn took the soul
Of that waste place with joy
Hidden in sorrow: at first to the ear
The warble was low, and full and clear;

And floating about the under-sky,
Prevailing in weakness, the coronach stole
Sometimes afar, and sometimes anear;
But anon her awful jubilant voice,
With a music strange and manifold,
Flow'd forth on a carol free and bold;
As when a mighty people rejoice
With shawms, and with cymbals, and harps of gold,

And the tumult of their acclaim is roll'd
Thro' the open gates of the city afar,
To the shepherd who watcheth the evening star.
And the creeping mosses and clambering weeds,
And the willow-branches hoar and dank,
And the wavy swell of the soughing reeds,
And the wave-worn horns of the echoing bank,
And the silvery marish-flowers that throng
The desolate creeks and pools among,
Were flooded over with eddying song.

24. Early Spring

Once more the Heavenly Power
Makes all things new,
And domes the red-plow'd hills
With loving blue;
The blackbirds have their wills,
The throstles too.

Opens a door in heaven;
From skies of glass
A Jacob's ladder falls
On greening grass,

And o'er the mountain-walls
Young angels pass.

Before them fleets the shower,
And burst the buds,
And shine the level lands,
And flash the floods;
The stars are from their hands
Flung thro' the woods,

The woods with living airs
How softly fann'd,
Light airs from where the deep,
All down the sand,
Is breathing in his sleep,
Heard by the land.

O, follow, leaping blood,
The season's lure!
O heart, look down and up
Serene, secure,
Warm as the crocus cup,
Like snowdrops, pure!

Past, Future glimpse and fade
Thro' some slight spell,
A gleam from yonder vale,
Some far blue fell,
And sympathies, how frail,
In sound and smell!

Till at thy chuckled note,
Thou twinkling bird,

The fairy fancies range,
And, lightly stirr'd,
Ring little bells of change
From word to word.

For now the Heavenly Power
Makes all things new,
And thaws the cold, and fills
The flower with dew;
The blackbirds have their wills,
The poets too.

25. England and America in 1782

John Hampden's arrest for resisting arbitrary taxes was the spark that started the First English Civil War in 1642 between Charles I and Oliver Cromwell.

O thou that sendest out the man
To rule by land and sea,
Strong mother of a Lion-line,
Be proud of those strong sons of thine
Who wrench'd their rights from thee!

What wonder if in noble heat
Those men thine arms withstood,
Retaught the lesson thou hadst taught,
And in thy spirit with thee fought
Who sprang from English blood!

But thou rejoice with liberal joy,
Lift up thy rocky face,
And shatter, when the storms are black,
In many a streaming torrent back,
The seas that shock thy base!

Whatever harmonies of law
The growing world assume,
Thy work is thine the single note
From that deep chord which Hampden smote
Will vibrate to the doom.

26. Far-far-away (For Music)

What sight so lured him thro' the fields he knew
As where earth's green stole into heaven's own hue,

Far-far-away?

What sound was dearest in his native dells?
The mellow lin-lan-lone of evening bells

Far-far-away.

What vague world-whisper, mystic pain or joy,
Thro' those three words would haunt him when a boy,

Far-far-away?

A whisper from his dawn of life? a breath
From some fair dawn beyond the doors of death

Far-far-away?

Far, far, how far? from o'er the gates of birth,
The faint horizons, all the bounds of earth,

Far-far-away?

What charm in words, a charm no words could give?
O dying words, can Music make you live

Far-far-away?

27. Flower in the Crannied Wall

Flower in the crannied wall,
I pluck you out of the crannies,
I hold you here, root and all, in my hand,
Little flower —but if I could understand
What you are, root and all, and all in all,
I should know what God and man is.

28. The May Queen

You must wake and call me early, call me early, mother dear;
To-morrow 'ill be the happiest time of all the glad New-year;
Of all the glad New-year, mother, the maddest merriest day,
For I'm to be Queen o' the May, mother, I'm to be Queen o' the
May.

There's many a black, black eye, they say, but none so bright as mine;
There's Margaret and Mary, there's Kate and Caroline;
But none so fair as little Alice in all the land they say,
So I'm to be Queen o' the May, mother, I'm to be Queen o' the May.

I sleep so sound all night, mother, that I shall never wake,
If you do not call me loud when the day begins to break;
But I must gather knots of flowers, and buds and garlands gay,
For I'm to be Queen o' the May, mother, I'm to be Queen o' the
May.

As I came up the valley whom think ye should I see
But Robin leaning on the bridge beneath the hazel-tree?
He thought of that sharp look, mother, I gave him yesterday,
But I'm to be Queen o' the May, mother, I'm to be Queen o' the
May.

He thought I was a ghost, mother, for I was all in white,
And I ran by him without speaking, like a flash of light.
They call me cruel-hearted, but I care not what they say,
For I'm to be Queen o' the May, mother, I'm to be Queen o' the
May.

They say he's dying all for love, but that can never be;
They say his heart is breaking, mother —what is that to me?
There's many a bolder lad 'ill woo me any summer day,
And I'm to be Queen o' the May, mother, I'm to be Queen o' the
May.

Little Effie shall go with me to-morrow to the green,
And you'll be there, too, mother, to see me made the Queen;
For the shepherd lads on every side 'ill come from far away,
And I'm to be Queen o' the May, mother, I'm to be Queen o' the
May.

The honeysuckle round the porch has woven its wavy bowers,
And by the meadow-trenches blow the faint sweet cuckoo-flowers;
And the wild marsh-marigold shines like fire in swamps and hollows
gray,
And I'm to be Queen o' the May, mother, I'm to be Queen o' the
May.

The night-winds come and go, mother, upon the meadow-grass,
And the happy stars above them seem to brighten as they pass;

There will not be a drop of rain the whole of the livelong day,
And I'm to be Queen o' the May, mother, I'm to be Queen o' the
May.

All the valley, mother, 'ill be fresh and green and still,
And the cowslip and the crowfoot are over all the hill,
And the rivulet in the flowery dale 'ill merrily glance and play,
For I'm to be Queen o' the May, mother, I'm to be Queen o' the
May.

So you must wake and call me early, call me early, mother dear,
To-morrow 'ill be the happiest time of all the glad New-year;
To-morrow 'ill be of all the year the maddest merriest day,
For I'm to be Queen o' the May, mother, I'm to be Queen o' the
May.

29. The Poet's Song

The rain had fallen, the Poet arose,
He pass'd by the town and out of the street;
A light wind blew from the gates of the sun,
And waves of shadow went over the wheat;
And he sat him down in a lonely place,
And chanted a melody loud and sweet,
That made the wild-swan pause in her cloud,
And the lark drop down at his feet.

The swallow stopt as he hunted the fly,
The snake slipt under a spray,
The wild hawk stood with the down on his beak,
And stared, with his foot on the prey;
And the nightingale thought, 'I have sung many songs,
But never a one so gay,

For he sings of what the world will be
When the years have died away.'

30. The Tears Of Heaven

Heaven weeps above the earth all night till morn,
In darkness weeps as all ashamed to weep,
Because the earth hath made her state forlorn
With self-wrought evil of unnumbered years,
And doth the fruit of her dishonor reap.
And all the day heaven gathers back her tears
Into her own blue eyes so clear and deep,
And showering down the glory of lightsome day,
Smiles on the earth's worn brow to win her if she may.

31. Will

O well for him whose will is strong!
He suffers, but he will not suffer long;
He suffers, but he cannot suffer wrong:
For him nor moves the loud world's random mock,
Nor all Calamity's hugest waves confound,
Who seems a promontory of rock,
That, compass'd round with turbulent sound,
In middle ocean meets the surging shock,
Tempest-buffeted, citadel-crown'd.

But ill for him who, bettering not with time,
Corrupts the strength of heaven-descended Will,
And ever weaker grows thro' acted crime,
Or seeming-genial venial fault,
Recurring and suggesting still!
He seems as one whose footsteps halt,
Toiling in immeasurable sand,

And o'er a weary sultry land,
Far beneath a blazing vault,
Sown in a wrinkle of the monstrous hill,
The city sparkles like a grain of salt.

32. The Throstle

"Summer is coming, summer is coming,
I know it, I know it, I know it.
Light again, leaf again, love again."
Yes, my wild little poet.

Sing the new year in under the blue,
Last year you sang it as gladly,
"New, new, new, new!" Is it then so new
That you should carol so madly?

"Love again, song again, nest again, young again,"
Never a prophet so crazy!
And hardly a daisy as yet, little friend,
See, there is hardly a daisy.

"Here again, here, here, here, happy year!"
O warble unchidden, unbidden!
Summer is coming, is coming, my dear.
And all the winters are hidden.

33. The City Child

Dainty little maiden, whither would you wander?
Whither from this pretty home, the home where mother dwells?
"Far and far away," said the dainty little maiden,
"All among the gardens, auriculas, anemones,
Roses and lilies and Canterbury-bells."

Dainty little maiden,whither would you wander?
Whither from this pretty house, this city-house of ours?
"Far and far away," said the dainty little maiden
"All among the meadows, the clover and the clematis,
Daisies and kingcups and honeysuckle flowers."

34. The Mermaid

Who would be
A mermaid fair,
Singing alone,
Combing her hair
Under the sea,
In a golden curl
With a comb of pearl,
On a throne?

I would be a mermaid fair;
I would sing to myself the whole of the day;
With a comb of pearl I would comb my hair;
And still as I comb'd I would sing and say,
'Who is it loves me? who loves not me?'
I would comb my hair till my ringlets would fall
Low adown, low adown,
From under my starry sea-bud crown
Low adown and around,
And I should look like a fountain of gold
Springing alone
With a shrill inner sound
Over the throne
In the midst of the hall;
Till that great sea-snake under the sea

From his coiled sleeps in the central deeps
Would slowly trail himself sevenfold
Round the hall where I sate, and look in at the gate
With his large calm eyes for the love of me.
And all the mermen under the sea
Would feel their immortality
Die in their hearts for the love of me.

But at night I would wander away, away,
I would fling on each side my low-flowing locks,
And lightly vault from the throne and play
With the mermen in and out of the rocks;
We would run to and fro, and hide and seek,
On the broad sea-wolds in the crimson shells,
Whose silvery spikes are nighest the sea.
But if any came near I would call and shriek,
And adown the steep like a wave I would leap
From the diamond-ledges that jut from the dells;
For I would not be kiss'd by all who would list
Of the bold merry mermen under the sea.
They would sue me, and woo me, and flatter me,
In the purple twilights under the sea;
But the king of them all would carry me,
Woo me, and win me, and marry me,
In the branching jaspers under the sea.
Then all the dry-pied things that be
In the hueless mosses under the sea
Would curl round my silver feet silently,
All looking up for the love of me.
And if I should carol aloud, from aloft
All things that are forked, and horned, and soft
Would lean out from the hollow sphere of the sea,
All looking down for the love of me.

35. The Owl

When cats run home and light is come,
And dew is cold upon the ground,
And the far-off stream is dumb,
And the whirring sail goes round,
And the whirring sail goes round;
Alone and warming his five wits,
The white owl in the belfry sits.

When merry milkmaids click the latch,
And rarely smells the new-mown hay,
And the cock hath sung beneath the thatch
Twice or thrice his roundelay,
Twice or thrice his roundelay;
Alone and warming his five wits,
The white owl in the belfry sits.

36. The Brook

Thorps are villages or hamlets.

I come from haunts of coot and hern,
I make a sudden sally,
And sparkle out among the fern,
To bicker down a valley.

By thirty hills I hurry down,
Or slip between the ridges,
By twenty thorps, a little town,
And half a hundred bridges.

Till last by Philip's farm I flow
To join the brimming river,

For men may come and men may go
But I go on forever.

I chatter over stony ways,
In little sharps and trebles,
I bubble into eddying bays,
I babble on the pebbles.

With many a curve my banks I fret,
By many a field and fallow,
And many a fairy foreland set
With willow-weed and mallow.

I chatter, chatter as I flow
To join the brimming river,
For men may come and men may go
But I go on forever.

I wind about, and in and out,
With here a blossom sailing,
And here and there a lusty trout,
And here and there a grayling.

And here and there a foamy flake
Upon me as I travel
With many a silver water-break
Above the golden gravel.

And draw them all along, and flow
To join the brimming river,
For men may come and men may go
But I go on forever.

I steal by lawns and grassy plots,
I slide by hazel covers;
I move the sweet forget-me-nots
That grow for happy lovers.

I slip, I slide, I gloom, I glance,
Among my skimming swallows;
I make the netted sunbeam dance
Against my sandy shallows.

I murmur under moon and stars
In brambly wildernesses;
I linger by my shingly bars;
I loiter round my cresses;

And out again I curve and flow
To join the brimming river,
For men may come and men may go
But I go on forever.

37. The Shell (from the longer work, "Maud")

See what a lovely shell,
Small and pure as a pearl,
Lying close to my foot,
Frail, but a work divine,
Made so fairily well
With delicate spire and whorl,
How exquisitely minute,
A miracle of design!

What is it? a learned man
Could give it a clumsy name.
Let him name it who can,
The beauty would be the same.

The tiny cell is forlorn,
Void of the little living will
That made it stir on the shore.
Did he stand at the diamond door
Of his house in a rainbow frill?
Did he push, when he was uncurl'd
A golden foot or fairy horn
Thro' his dim water-world?

Slight, to be crush'd with a tap
Of my finger-nail on the sand;
Small, but a work divine,
Frail, but of force to withstand,
Year upon year, the shock
Of cataract seas that snap
The three-decker's oaken spine
Athwart the ledges of rock,
Here on the Breton strand!

38. Lady Clare

It was the time when lilies blow,
    And clouds are highest up in air,
Lord Ronald brought a lily-white doe
    To give his cousin, Lady Clare.

I trow they did not part in scorn —
    Lovers long-betroth'd were they:

They too will wed the morrow morn:
    God's blessing on the day!

'He does not love me for my birth,
    Nor for my lands so broad and fair;
He loves me for my own true worth,
    And that is well,' said Lady Clare.

In there came old Alice the nurse,
    Said, 'Who was this that went from thee?'
'It was my cousin,' said Lady Clare,
    'To-morrow he weds with me.'

'O God be thank'd!' said Alice the nurse,
    'That all comes round so just and fair:
Lord Ronald is heir of all your lands,
    And you are not the Lady Clare.'

'Are ye out of your mind, my nurse, my nurse?'
    Said Lady Clare, 'that ye speak so wild?'
'As God's above,' said Alice the nurse,
    'I speak the truth: you are my child.

'The old Earl's daughter died at my breast;
    I speak the truth, as I live by bread!
I buried her like my own sweet child,
    And put my child in her stead.'

'Falsely, falsely have ye done,
    O mother,' she said, 'if this be true,
To keep the best man under the sun
    So many years from his due.'

'Nay now, my child,' said Alice the nurse,
    'But keep the secret for your life,
And all you have will be Lord Ronald's,
    When you are man and wife.'

'If I'm a beggar born,' she said,
    'I will speak out, for I dare not lie.
Pull off, pull off, the brooch of gold,
    And fling the diamond necklace by.'

'Nay now, my child,' said Alice the nurse,
    'But keep the secret all ye can.'
She said, 'Not so: but I will know
    If there be any faith in man.'

'Nay now, what faith?' said Alice the nurse,
    'The man will cleave unto his right.'
'And he shall have it,' the lady replied,
    'Tho' I should die to-night.'

'Yet give one kiss to your mother dear !
    Alas, my child, I sinn'd for thee.'
'O mother, mother, mother,' she said,
    'So strange it seems to me.

'Yet here's a kiss for my mother dear,
    My mother dear, if this be so,
And lay your hand upon my head,
    And bless me, mother, ere I go.'

She clad herself in a russet gown,
    She was no longer Lady Clare:
She went by dale, and she went by down,

With a single rose in her hair.

The lily-white doe Lord Ronald had brought
    Leapt up from where she lay,
Dropt her head in the maiden's hand,
    And follow'd her all the way.

Down stept Lord Ronald from his tower:
    'O Lady Clare, you shame your worth!
Why come you drest like a village maid,
    That are the flower of the earth?'

'If I come drest like a village maid,
    I am but as my fortunes are:
I am a beggar born,' she said,
    'And not the Lady Clare.'

'Play me no tricks,' said Lord Ronald,
    'For I am yours in word and in deed.
Play me no tricks,' said Lord Ronald,
    'Your riddle is hard to read.'

O and proudly stood she up!
    Her heart within her did not fail:
She look'd into Lord Ronald's eyes,
    And told him all her nurse's tale.

He laugh'd a laugh of merry scorn:
    He turn'd and kiss'd her where she stood:
'If you are not the heiress born,
    And I,' said he, 'the next in blood –

'If you are not the heiress born,

And I,' said he, 'the lawful heir,
We two will wed to-morrow morn,
    And you shall still be Lady Clare.'

39. The Lady of Shalott

On either side the river lie
Long fields of barley and of rye,
That clothe the wold and meet the sky;
And thro' the field the road runs by
To many-tower'd Camelot;
And up and down the people go,
Gazing where the lilies blow
Round an island there below,
The island of Shalott.

Willows whiten, aspens quiver,
Little breezes dusk and shiver
Through the wave that runs for ever
By the island in the river
Flowing down to Camelot.
Four grey walls, and four grey towers,
Overlook a space of flowers,
And the silent isle imbowers
The Lady of Shalott.

By the margin, willow veil'd,
Slide the heavy barges trail'd
By slow horses; and unhail'd
The shallop flitteth silken-sail'd
Skimming down to Camelot:
But who hath seen her wave her hand?
Or at the casement seen her stand?

Or is she known in all the land,
The Lady of Shalott?

Only reapers, reaping early,
In among the bearded barley
Hear a song that echoes cheerly
From the river winding clearly;
Down to tower'd Camelot;
And by the moon the reaper weary,
Piling sheaves in uplands airy,
Listening, whispers, "'Tis the fairy
Lady of Shalott."

There she weaves by night and day
A magic web with colours gay.
She has heard a whisper say,
A curse is on her if she stay
To look down to Camelot.
She knows not what the curse may be,
And so she weaveth steadily,
And little other care hath she,
The Lady of Shalott.

And moving through a mirror clear
That hangs before her all the year,
Shadows of the world appear.
There she sees the highway near
Winding down to Camelot;
There the river eddy whirls,
And there the surly village churls,
And the red cloaks of market girls
Pass onward from Shalott.

Sometimes a troop of damsels glad,
An abbot on an ambling pad,
Sometimes a curly shepherd lad,
Or long-hair'd page in crimson clad
Goes by to tower'd Camelot;
And sometimes through the mirror blue
The knights come riding two and two.
She hath no loyal Knight and true,
The Lady of Shalott.

But in her web she still delights
To weave the mirror's magic sights,
For often through the silent nights
A funeral, with plumes and lights
And music, went to Camelot;
Or when the Moon was overhead,
Came two young lovers lately wed.
"I am half sick of shadows," said
The Lady of Shalott.

A bow-shot from her bower-eaves,
He rode between the barley sheaves,
The sun came dazzling thro' the leaves,
And flamed upon the brazen greaves
Of bold Sir Lancelot.
A red-cross knight for ever kneel'd
To a lady in his shield,
That sparkled on the yellow field,
Beside remote Shalott.

The gemmy bridle glitter'd free,
Like to some branch of stars we see
Hung in the golden Galaxy.

The bridle bells rang merrily
As he rode down to Camelot:
And from his blazon'd baldric slung
A mighty silver bugle hung,
And as he rode his armor rung
Beside remote Shalott.

All in the blue unclouded weather
Thick-jewell'd shone the saddle-leather,
The helmet and the helmet-feather
Burn'd like one burning flame together,
As he rode down to Camelot.
As often thro' the purple night,
Below the starry clusters bright,
Some bearded meteor, burning bright,
Moves over still Shalott.

His broad clear brow in sunlight glow'd;
On burnish'd hooves his war-horse trode;
From underneath his helmet flow'd
His coal-black curls as on he rode,
As he rode down to Camelot.
From the bank and from the river
He flashed into the crystal mirror,
"Tirra lirra," by the river
Sang Sir Lancelot.

She left the web, she left the loom,
She made three paces through the room,
She saw the water-lily bloom,
She saw the helmet and the plume,
She look'd down to Camelot.
Out flew the web and floated wide;

The mirror crack'd from side to side;
"The curse is come upon me," cried
The Lady of Shalott.

In the stormy east-wind straining,
The pale yellow woods were waning,
The broad stream in his banks complaining.
Heavily the low sky raining
Over tower'd Camelot;
Down she came and found a boat
Beneath a willow left afloat,
And around about the prow she wrote
The Lady of Shalott.

And down the river's dim expanse
Like some bold seer in a trance,
Seeing all his own mischance —
With a glassy countenance
Did she look to Camelot.
And at the closing of the day
She loosed the chain, and down she lay;
The broad stream bore her far away,
The Lady of Shalott.

Lying, robed in snowy white
That loosely flew to left and right —
The leaves upon her falling light —
Thro' the noises of the night,
She floated down to Camelot:
And as the boat-head wound along
The willowy hills and fields among,
They heard her singing her last song,
The Lady of Shalott.

Heard a carol, mournful, holy,
Chanted loudly, chanted lowly,
Till her blood was frozen slowly,
And her eyes were darkened wholly,
Turn'd to tower'd Camelot.
For ere she reach'd upon the tide
The first house by the water-side,
Singing in her song she died,
The Lady of Shalott.

Under tower and balcony,
By garden-wall and gallery,
A gleaming shape she floated by,
Dead-pale between the houses high,
Silent into Camelot.
Out upon the wharfs they came,
Knight and Burgher, Lord and Dame,
And around the prow they read her name,
The Lady of Shalott.

Who is this? And what is here?
And in the lighted palace near
Died the sound of royal cheer;
And they crossed themselves for fear,
All the Knights at Camelot;
But Lancelot mused a little space
He said, "She has a lovely face;
God in his mercy lend her grace,
The Lady of Shalott."

40. Crossing the Bar

Sunset and evening star,
    And one clear call for me!
And may there be no moaning of the bar,
    When I put out to sea,

But such a tide as moving seems asleep,
    Too full for sound or foam,
When that which drew from out the boundless deep
    Turns again home.

Twilight and evening bell,
    And after that the dark!
And may there be no sadness of farewell;
    When I embark;

For tho' from out our bourne of Time and Place
    The flood may bear me far,
I hope to see my pilot face to face
    When I have crossed the bar.

Emily Dickinson (1830-1886)

Biographical Sketch by Donna-Jean Breckenridge

> "There is no Frigate like a Book to take us Lands away…"

Yes! my young heart thought. That's it, exactly! But wait —what's a frigate?

"As imperceptibly as grief the summer passed away," and I nodded in mournful agreement. "Too imperceptible, at last, to seem like perfidy." Hold on —what is perfidy?

"A route of evanescence with a revolving wheel; a resonance of emerald," and I could picture it, this tiny bird in its beauty. I loved the sound and feel of the words, and then I read "a rush of cochineal."

And once more, Emily Dickinson sent me off to a dictionary.

But what sets Dickinson's writing apart is far more than a random, obscure vocabulary word.

The cover of my small *Everyman's Library Pocket Poets* book expressed it well. "Virtually unknown as a poet in her lifetime, Emily Dickinson is now recognized as one of the most unaccountably strange and marvelous of the world's great writers." Strange and marvelous. And that's just part of the lure.

"Her poems," it went on, "represent a mind unlike any other to be found in literature."

Emily Dickinson's grandfather was one of the founders of Amherst College. Her father was the college treasurer and later became a United States Congressman. Emily Dickinson herself was very well-read, and she was influenced by the Bible, William Wordsworth, Charlotte Brontë, Ralph Waldo Emerson, and especially Shakespeare. After attending Amherst Academy and the Mount Holyoke Female Seminary, Emily Dickinson began a quiet life at home. With the exception of a trip to Philadelphia and Washington, D.C., and also two trips to Boston for her health, Dickinson never left Amherst. More than that, she became a recluse and seldom left the confines of her own home.

But she wrote. She wrote hundreds of letters, and her recipients included friends, relatives, and even a publisher. But mainly she wrote poems.

Dickinson's poetry, though penned by a woman who never married, eschewed social settings, and did not travel, covered the fathomless mysteries of nature and the full range of human emotion. And in her bold and daring look at life, she wrote about both doubt and hope, love and fear, friendship and isolation, life and death. And she did it all, using uncommon capitalization and a liberal use of dashes.

In one of her last poems, she wrote,

"Of God we ask one favor,
That we may be forgiven —
For what, he is presumed to know –
The crime, from us is hidden —
Immured, the whole of life
Within a magic Prison
We reprimand the Happiness
That too competes with Heaven."

During her life, few knew that she did much more than care for her aging parents. A couple poems were published anonymously, but it was not until after her death that the scope of her writing was discovered. Her younger sister Lavinia found a collection of nearly 1800 poems. The woman who once wrote "I'm Nobody! Who are you?" has remained continuously in print since 1880.

"If my Bark sink
'Tis to another sea —
Mortality's Ground Floor
Is Immortality —"

01. I Never Saw a Moor

I never saw a moor,
I never saw the sea;
Yet know I how the heather looks,
And what a wave must be.

I never spoke with God,
Nor visited in heaven;
Yet certain am I of the spot
As if the chart were given.

02. The Lost Jewel

I held a jewel in my fingers
And went to sleep.
The day was warm, and winds were prosy;
I said: "'T'will keep."

I woke and chid my honest fingers,
The gem was gone;
And now an amethyst remembrance
Is all I own.

03. A Book

There is no Frigate like a Book
To take us Lands away
Nor any Coursers like a Page
Of prancing Poetry —
This Traverse may the poorest take
Without oppress of Toll —
How frugal is the Chariot
That bears the Human Soul —

04. The Wind's Visit

The wind tapped like a tired man,
And like a host, "Come in,"
I boldly answered; entered then
My residence within

A rapid, footless guest,
To offer whom a chair
Were as impossible as hand
A sofa to the air.

No bone had he to bind him,
His speech was like the push
Of numerous humming-birds at once
From a superior bush.

His countenance a billow,
His fingers, if he pass,
Let go a music, as of tunes
Blown tremulous in glass.

He visited, still flitting;
Then, like a timid man,
Again he tapped 't was flurriedly
And I became alone.

05. A Thunder-Storm

The Wind begun to rock the Grass
With threatening Tunes and low —
He threw a Menace at the Earth —
A Menace at the Sky.

The Leaves unhooked themselves from Trees —
And started all abroad
The Dust did scoop itself like Hands
And threw away the Road.

The Wagons quickened on the Streets
The Thunder hurried slow —
The Lightning showed a Yellow Beak
And then a livid Claw.

The Birds put up the Bars to Nests —
The Cattle fled to Barns —
There came one drop of Giant Rain
And then as if the Hands

That held the Dams had parted hold
The Waters Wrecked the Sky,
But overlooked my Father's House —
Just quartering a Tree —

06. Beclouded

The Sky is low — the Clouds are mean.
A Travelling Flake of Snow
Across a Barn or through a Rut
Debates if it will go —

A Narrow Wind complains all Day
How some one treated him
Nature, like Us is sometimes caught
Without her Diadem.

07. Summer Shower

A Drop Fell on the Apple Tree —
Another — on the Roof —
A Half a Dozen kissed the Eaves —
And made the Gables laugh —

A few went out to help the Brook
That went to help the Sea —
Myself Conjectured were they Pearls —
What Necklace could be —

The Dust replaced, in Hoisted Roads —
The Birds jocoser sung —
The Sunshine threw his Hat away —
The Bushes — spangles flung —

The Breezes brought dejected Lutes —
And bathed them in the Glee —
Then Orient showed a single Flag,
And signed the Fete away —

08. If I Can Stop One Heart From Breaking

If I can stop one heart from breaking,
I shall not live in vain;
If I can ease one life the aching,
Or cool one pain,
Or help one fainting robin
Unto his nest again,
I shall not live in vain.

09. A Word

A word is dead
When it is said,
Some say.
I say it just
Begins to live
That day.

10. The Railway Train

Boanerges, in the Victorian era, referred to loud preachers.

I like to see it lap the Miles —
And lick the Valleys up —
And stop to feed itself at Tanks —
And then — prodigious step

Around a Pile of Mountains —
And supercilious peer
In Shanties — by the sides of Roads —
And then a Quarry pare

To fit its Ribs
And crawl between
Complaining all the while
In horrid — hooting stanza —
Then chase itself down Hill —

And neigh like Boanerges —
Then — punctual as a Star
Stop — docile and omnipotent
At its own stable door —

11. The Bee is Not Afraid of Me

The bee is not afraid of me,
I know the butterfly;
The pretty people in the woods
Receive me cordially.

The brooks laugh louder when I come,
The breezes madder play.
Wherefore, mine eyes, thy silver mists?
Wherefore, O summer's day?

12. As Children Bid the Guest Goodnight

As children bid the guest good-night,
And then reluctant turn,
My flowers raise their pretty lips,
Then put their nightgowns on.

As children caper when they wake,
Merry that it is morn,
My flowers from a hundred cribs
Will peep, and prance again.

13. A Day

I'll tell you how the Sun rose —
A Ribbon at a time —
The Steeples swam in Amethyst —
The news, like Squirrels, ran —
The Hills untied their Bonnets —
The Bobolinks — begun —
Then I said softly to myself —

"That must have been the Sun"!
But how he set — I know not —
There seemed a purple stile
That little Yellow boys and girls
Were climbing all the while —
Till when they reached the other side,
A Dominie in Gray —
Put gently up the evening Bars —
And led the flock away —

14. The Pedigree of Honey

The pedigree of honey
Does not concern the bee;
A clover, any time, to him
Is aristocracy.

15. The Grass

The Grass so little has to do —
A Sphere of simple Green —
With only Butterflies to brood
And Bees to entertain —

And stir all day to pretty Tunes
The Breezes fetch along —
And hold the Sunshine in its lap
And bow to everything —

And thread the Dews, all night, like Pearls —
And make itself so fine
A Duchess were too common
For such a noticing —

And even when it dies — to pass
In Odors so divine —
Like Lowly spices, lain to sleep —
Or Spikenards, perishing —

And then, in Sovereign Barns to dwell —
And dream the Days away,
The Grass so little has to do
I wish I were a Hay —

16. Perhaps You'd Like to Buy a Flower

Perhaps you'd like to buy a flower?
But I could never sell.
If you would like to borrow
Until the daffodil

Unties her yellow bonnet
Beneath the village door,
Until the bees, from clover rows
Their hock and sherry draw,

Why, I will lend until just then,
But not an hour more!

17. The Moon

The Moon was but a Chin of Gold
A Night or two ago —
And now she turns Her perfect Face
Upon the World below —

Her Forehead is of Amplest Blonde —
Her Cheek — a Beryl hewn —
Her Eye unto the Summer Dew
The likest I have known —

Her Lips of Amber never part —
But what must be the smile
Upon Her Friend she could confer
Were such Her Silver Will —

And what a privilege to be
But the remotest Star —
For Certainty She take Her Way
Beside Your Palace Door —

Her Bonnet is the Firmament —
The Universe — Her Shoe —
The Stars — the Trinkets at Her Belt —
Her Dimities — of Blue —

18. Evening

The Crickets sang
And set the Sun
And Workmen finished one by one
Their Seam the Day upon.

The low Grass loaded with the Dew
The Twilight stood, as Strangers do
With Hat in Hand, polite and new
To stay as if, or go.

A Vastness, as a Neighbor, came,
A Wisdom, without Face, or Name,
A Peace, as Hemispheres at Home
And so the Night became.

19. Autumn

The morns are meeker than they were —
The nuts are getting brown —
The berry's cheek is plumper —
The Rose is out of town.

The Maple wears a gayer scarf —
The field a scarlet gown —
Lest I should be old fashioned
I'll put a trinket on.

20. The Butterfly's Day

From Cocoon forth a Butterfly
As Lady from her Door
Emerged — a Summer Afternoon —
Repairing Everywhere —

Without Design — that I could trace
Except to stray abroad
On Miscellaneous Enterprise
The Clovers — understood —

Her pretty Parasol be seen
Contracting in a Field

Where Men made Hay ——
Then struggling hard
With an opposing Cloud ——

Where Parties —— Phantom as Herself ——
To Nowhere —— seemed to go
In purposeless Circumference ——
As 'twere a Tropic Show ——

And notwithstanding Bee —— that worked ——
And Flower —— that zealous blew ——
This Audience of Idleness
Disdained them, from the Sky ——

Till Sundown crept —— a steady Tide ——
And Men that made the Hay ——
And Afternoon —— and Butterfly ——
Extinguished —— in the Sea ——

21. Fringed Gentian

God made a little Gentian ——
It tried —— to be a Rose ——
And failed —— and all the Summer laughed ——
But just before the Snows

There rose a Purple Creature ——
That ravished all the Hill ——
And Summer hid her Forehead ——
And Mockery —— was still ——

The Frosts were her condition ——

The Tyrian would not come
Until the North — invoke it —
Creator — Shall I — bloom?

22. The Snow

It sifts from Leaden Sieves —
It powders all the Wood.
It fills with Alabaster Wool
The Wrinkles of the Road —

It makes an Even Face
Of Mountain, and of Plain —
Unbroken Forehead from the East
Unto the East again —

It reaches to the Fence —
It wraps it Rail by Rail
Till it is lost in Fleeces —
It deals Celestial Vail

To Stump, and Stack — and Stem —
A Summer's empty Room —
Acres of Joints, where Harvests were,
Recordless, but for them —

It Ruffles Wrists of Posts
As Ankles of a Queen —
Then stills its Artisans — like Ghosts —
Denying they have been —

23. The Sea

An Everywhere of Silver
With Ropes of Sand
To keep it from effacing
The Track called Land.

24. Forbidden Fruit

"Heaven" — is what I cannot reach!
The Apple on the Tree —
Provided it do hopeless — hang —
That — "Heaven" is — to Me!

The Color, on the Cruising Cloud —
The interdicted Land —
Behind the Hill — the House behind —
There — Paradise — is found!

Her teasing Purples — Afternoons —
The credulous — decoy —
Enamored — of the Conjurer —
That spurned us — Yesterday!

25. The Woodpecker

His Bill an Auger is
His Head, a Cap and Frill
He laboreth at every Tree
A Worm, His utmost Goal.

26. Hope

"Hope" is the thing with feathers —
That perches in the soul —
And sings the tune without the words —
And never stops — at all —

And sweetest — in the Gale — is heard —
And sore must be the storm —
That could abash the little Bird
That kept so many warm —

I've heard it in the chillest land —
And on the strangest Sea —
Yet — never — in Extremity,
It asked a crumb — of me.

27. May-flower

Pink — small — and punctual —
Aromatic — low —
Covert — in April —
Candid — in May —
Dear to the Moss —
Known to the Knoll —
Next to the Robin
In every human Soul —
Bold little Beauty
Bedecked with thee
Nature forswears
Antiquity —

28. Old-Fashioned

"Arcturus" is his other name —
I'd rather call him "Star."
It's very mean of Science
To go and interfere!

I slew a worm the other day —
A "Savant" passing by
Murmured "Resurgam" — "Centipede"!
"Oh Lord — how frail are we"!

I pull a flower from the woods —
A monster with a glass
Computes the stamens in a breath —
And has her in a "class"!

Whereas I took the Butterfly
Aforetime in my hat —
He sits erect in "Cabinets" —
The Clover bells forgot.

What once was "Heaven" Is "Zenith" now —
Where I proposed to go
When Time's brief masquerade was done
Is mapped and charted too.

What if the poles should frisk about
And stand upon their heads!
I hope I'm ready for "the worst" —
Whatever prank betides!

Perhaps the "Kingdom of Heaven's" changed —
I hope the "Children" there
Won't be "new fashioned" when I come —
And laugh at me — and stare —

I hope the Father in the skies

Will lift his little girl —
Old fashioned — naught — everything —
Over the stile of "Pearl."

29. Have You Got a Brook in your Little Heart

Have you got a brook in your little heart,
Where bashful flowers blow,
And blushing birds go down to drink,
And shadows tremble so?

And nobody knows, so still it flows,
That any brook is there;
And yet your little draught of life
Is daily drunken there.

Then look out for the little brook in March,
When the rivers overflow,
And the snows come hurrying from the hills,
And the bridges often go.

And later, in August it may be,
When the meadows parching lie,
Beware, lest this little brook of life
Some burning noon go dry!

30. Dawn

Not knowing when the Dawn will come,
I open every Door,
Or has it Feathers, like a Bird,
Or Billows, like a Shore —

31. A Service of Song

Some keep the Sabbath going to Church —
I keep it, staying at Home —
With a Bobolink for a Chorister —
And an Orchard, for a Dome —

Some keep the Sabbath in Surplice —
I just wear my Wings —
And instead of tolling the Bell, for Church,
Our little Sexton — sings.

God preaches, a noted Clergyman —
And the sermon is never long,
So instead of getting to Heaven, at last —
I'm going, all along.

32. Who Has Not Found the Heaven Below

Who has not found the Heaven — below —
Will fail of it above —
For Angels rent the House next ours,
Wherever we remove —

33. Proof

That I did always love
I bring thee Proof
That till I loved
I never lived — Enough —

That I shall love alway —
I argue thee
That love is life —
And life hath Immortality —

This — dost thou doubt — Sweet —
Then have I
Nothing to show
But Calvary —

34. I'm Nobody! Who Are You?

I'm Nobody! Who are you?
Are you — Nobody — too?
Then there's a pair of us!
Don't tell! they'd advertise — you know.

How dreary — to be — Somebody!
How public — like a Frog —
To tell one's name — the livelong June —
To an admiring Bog!

35. Nature is What we See

"Nature" is what we see —
The Hill — the Afternoon —
Squirrel — Eclipse — the Bumble bee —
Nay — Nature is Heaven —
Nature is what we hear —
The Bobolink — the Sea —
Thunder — the Cricket —
Nay — Nature is Harmony —
Nature is what we know —
Yet have no art to say —
So impotent Our Wisdom is
To her Simplicity.

36. Sweet is the Swamp With its Secrets

Sweet is the swamp with its secrets,
Until we meet a snake;
'T is then we sigh for houses,
And our departure take

At that enthralling gallop
That only childhood knows.
A snake is summer's treason,
And guile is where it goes.

37. The Duties of the Wind are Few

The duties of the Wind are few,
To cast the ships, at Sea,
Establish March, the Floods escort,
And usher Liberty.

38. The Robin is the One

The Robin is the One
That interrupt the Morn
With hurried — few — express Reports
When March is scarcely on —

The Robin is the One
That overflow the Noon
With her cherubic quantity —
An April but begun —

The Robin is the One
That speechless from her Nest
Submit that Home — and Certainty
And Sanctity, are best

39. How Still the Bells in Steeples Stand

How still the Bells in Steeples stand
Till swollen with the Sky
They leap upon their silver Feet
In frantic Melody!

40. A Slash of Blue

A slash of Blue —
A sweep of Gray —
Some scarlet patches on the way,
Compose an Evening Sky —
A little purple — slipped between —
Some Ruby Trousers hurried on —
A Wave of Gold —
A Bank of Day —
This just makes out the Morning Sky.

41. The Saddest Noise, the Sweetest Noise

The saddest noise, the sweetest noise,
   The maddest noise that grows, —
The birds, they make it in the spring,
   At night's delicious close.

Between the March and April line —
   That magical frontier
Beyond which summer hesitates,
   Almost too heavenly near.

It makes us think of all the dead
   That sauntered with us here,
By separation's sorcery
   Made cruelly more dear.

It makes us think of what we had,
   And what we now deplore.
We almost wish those siren throats
   Would go and sing no more.

An ear can break a human heart
    As quickly as a spear,
We wish the ear had not a heart
    So dangerously near.

42. This Is My Letter To the World

This is my letter to the World
That never wrote to Me —
The simple News that Nature told —
With tender Majesty

Her Message is committed
To Hands I cannot see —
For love of Her — Sweet — countrymen —
Judge tenderly — of Me

43. Morning

Will there really be a "Morning"?
Is there such a thing as "Day"?
Could I see it from the mountains
If I were as tall as they?

Has it feet like Water lilies?
Has it feathers like a Bird?
Is it brought from famous countries
Of which I have never heard?

Oh some Scholar! Oh some Sailor!
Oh some Wise Men from the skies!

Please to tell a little Pilgrim
Where the place called "Morning" lies!

44. The Hummingbird

A Route of Evanescence
With a revolving Wheel —
A Resonance of Emerald —
A Rush of Cochineal —
And every Blossom on the Bush
Adjusts its tumbled Head —
The mail from Tunis, probably,
An easy Morning's Ride —

45. The Snake

A narrow Fellow in the Grass
Occasionally rides —
You may have met Him — did you not
His notice sudden is —

The Grass divides as with a Comb —
A spotted shaft is seen —
And then it closes at your feet
And opens further on —

He likes a Boggy Acre
A Floor too cool for Corn —
Yet when a Boy, and Barefoot —
I more than once at Noon

Have passed, I thought, a Whip lash

Unbraiding in the Sun
When stooping to secure it
It wrinkled and was gone —

Several of Nature's People
I know, and they know me —
I feel for them a transport
Of cordiality —

But never met this Fellow,
Attended, or alone
Without a tighter breathing
And Zero at the Bone —

46. Indian Summer

These are the days when Birds come back —
A very few — a Bird or two —
To take a backward look.

These are the days when skies resume
The old — old sophistries of June —
A blue and gold mistake.

Oh fraud that cannot cheat the Bee —
Almost thy plausibility
Induces my belief.

Till ranks of seeds their witness bear —
And softly thro' the altered air
Hurries a timid leaf.

Oh Sacrament of summer days,
Oh Last Communion in the Haze —
Permit a child to join.

Thy sacred emblems to partake —
They consecrated bread to take
And thine immortal wine!

William Wordsworth (1770-1850)

"Many of us will feel that Wordsworth is the poet to read, and grow thereby. He, almost more than any other English poet of the last century, has proved himself a power, and a power for good, making for whatever is true, pure, simple, teachable; for what is supersensuous, at any rate, if not spiritual."
(Charlotte Mason, *Formation of Character*, p. 225)

"A Heart That Watches and Receives": Biographical Sketch by Donna-Jean Breckenridge

Wordsworth.

Just think of it! A poet whose name evokes what he does, in that he takes words and makes them worthy. Wordsworth means the Lake District, a sleep and a forgetting, first-born affinities, the child is father of the man, a violet in a mossy stone, and always, a host of golden daffodils. Wordsworth's poetry includes approachable nature, recognizable emotions, and a picture of the relationship between the two. And sometimes he does it all "within the sonnet's scanty ground."

William Wordsworth was born in Cockermouth, England, in 1770, in what is now referred to as Cumbria, in the scenic Lake District. He was the second of five children; his sister Dorothy, a poet in her own right, was born just a year after William and they were close all their lives. Their father, whose job took him away from the family for long stretches of time, provided his children with a home that included a library and a situation beside the Derwent River. So William grew up with access to great books and a rural paradise, and his poetry reflected that.

However, William's mother Ann's death in 1778 disrupted their home, and Dorothy was sent away to live with a series of relatives. William and Dorothy were not reunited for nine years. In the meantime, his schooling continued, culminating with a tour of the Alps before his final year as a sizar at St. John's College (a sizar was someone who received financial help).

It was during that and a subsequent trip to the Continent that Wordsworth felt a passion for the French Revolution, democracy, and a woman named Annette. And it was these trips that furthered the poetry he had already begun to write in his earlier years. Once back in England, a chance meeting shaped the course of Wordsworth's life and poetry —for it was there that William and Dorothy met Samuel Taylor Coleridge.

Wordsworth and Coleridge inspired each other, critiqued each other's work, and eventually published "Lyrical Ballads" together, a collection of poems considered as the beginning of the Romantic Era. The two men, along with mutual friend Robert Southey, came to be known as the "Lake Poets."

A positive change in financial stability allowed William to marry Mary Hutchinson in 1802, and they had five children, of which two died in childhood. Wordsworth's writing in these years included the well-known "Ode: Intimations of Immortality from Recollections of Early Childhood." Charlotte Mason, in "Home Education," called this "that great ode, which next after the Bible, shows the deepest insight into what is peculiar to the children in their nature and estate."

He also continued work on an autobiographical poem later named *The Prelude*, though it was never named as such by Wordsworth himself. He and his family referred to it as "the poem to Coleridge," "the poem on his own early life," or (in a letter to T.N. Talfourd, dated April 11, 1839) "a long poem upon the formation of my own mind." Today we speak of the 1805 and the 1850 *Prelude*, the first and last versions of its complete text. Mary Wordsworth published it a few months after William's death; it is considered his *magnum opus* (most important work).

William Wordsworth was named Poet Laureate of England in 1843, and he died in 1850.

Note: The extensive notes included for these poems are based on Wordsworth's own work, but have been adapted for modern readers.

01. Lines Written in Early Spring

Wordsworth wrote this poem while sitting in a favorite spot, by a brook that "fell down a sloping rock so as to make a waterfall considerable for that country, and across the pool below had fallen a tree, an ash if I rightly remember, from which rose perpendicularly, boughs in search of the light intercepted by the deep shade above. The boughs bore leaves of green that for want of sunshine had faded into almost lily-white; and from the underside of this natural sylvan bridge depended long and beautiful tresses of ivy which waved gently in the breeze that might poetically speaking be called the breath of the waterfall."

I heard a thousand blended notes,
While in a grove I sate reclined,
In that sweet mood when pleasant thoughts
Bring sad thoughts to the mind.

To her fair works did Nature link
The human soul that through me ran;
And much it grieved my heart to think
What man has made of man.

Through primrose tufts, in that green bower,
The periwinkle trailed its wreaths;
And 'tis my faith that every flower
Enjoys the air it breathes.

The birds around me hopped and played,
Their thoughts I cannot measure —
But the least motion which they made,
It seemed a thrill of pleasure.

The budding twigs spread out their fan,
To catch the breezy air;
And I must think, do all I can,
That there was pleasure there.

If this belief from heaven be sent,
If such be Nature's holy plan,
Have I not reason to lament
What man has made of man?

02. Written in March

Wordsworth wrote this poem "while resting on the bridge at the foot of Brother's Water." He then added the word "Extempore," which meant that he had written it without any preparation, in the same way that an artist does a quick sketch.

    The Cock is crowing,
    The stream is flowing,
    The small birds twitter,
    The lake doth glitter,
The green field sleeps in the sun;
    The oldest and youngest
    Are at work with the strongest;
    The cattle are grazing,
    Their heads never raising;
There are forty feeding like one!

    Like an army defeated
    The snow hath retreated,
    And now doth fare ill
    On the top of the bare hill;
The ploughboy is whooping —anon —anon:
    There's joy in the mountains;

There's life in the fountains;
　　Small clouds are sailing,
　　Blue sky prevailing;
The rain is over and gone!

03. The Kitten and the Falling Leaves

Composed in 1804. Wordsworth included this note: "Seen at Town-end, Grasmere. The elder-bush has long since disappeared: it hung over the wall near the Cottage, and the Kitten continued to leap up, catching the leaves as here described. The infant was Dora." [His daughter Dora was born in 1804].

That way look, my Infant, lo!
What a pretty baby-show!
See the Kitten on the wall,
Sporting with the leaves that fall,
Withered leaves —one —two —and three —
From the lofty elder-tree!
Through the calm and frosty air
Of this morning bright and fair,
Eddying round and round they sink
Softly, slowly: one might think,
From the motions that are made,
Every little leaf conveyed
Sylph or Faery hither tending, —
To this lower world descending,
Each invisible and mute,
In his wavering parachute.
　—But the Kitten, how she starts,
Crouches, stretches, paws, and darts!
First at one, and then its fellow
Just as light and just as yellow;
There are many now —now one —

Now they stop and there are none.
What intenseness of desire
In her upward eye of fire!
With a tiger-leap half-way
Now she meets the coming prey,
Lets it go as fast, and then
Has it in her power again:
Now she works with three or four,
Like an Indian conjurer;
Quick as he in feats of art,
Far beyond in joy of heart.
Were her antics played in the eye
Of a thousand standers-by,
Clapping hands with shout and stare,
What would little Tabby care
For the plaudits of the crowd?
Over happy to be proud,
Over wealthy in the treasure
Of her own exceeding pleasure!
'Tis a pretty baby-treat;
Nor, I deem, for me unmeet;
Here, for neither Babe nor me,
Other play-mate can I see.
Of the countless living things,
That with stir of feet and wings
(In the sun or under shade,
Upon bough or grassy blade)
And with busy revellings,
Chirp and song, and murmurings,
Made this orchard's narrow space,
And this vale so blithe a place;
Multitudes are swept away
Never more to breathe the day:

Some are sleeping; some in bands
Travelled into distant lands;
Others slunk to moor and wood,
Far from human neighbourhood;
And, among the Kinds that keep
With us closer fellowship,
With us openly abide,
All have laid their mirth aside.
Where is he that giddy Sprite,
Blue-cap, with his colours bright,
Who was blest as bird could be,
Feeding in the apple-tree;
Made such wanton spoil and rout,
Turning blossoms inside out;
Hung-head pointing towards the ground —
Fluttered, perched, into a round
Bound himself, and then unbound;
Lithest, gaudiest Harlequin!
Prettiest Tumbler ever seen!
Light of heart and light of limb;
What is now become of Him?
Lambs, that through the mountains went
Frisking, bleating merriment,
When the year was in its prime,
They are sobered by this time.
If you look to vale or hill,
If you listen, all is still,
Save a little neighbouring rill,
That from out the rocky ground
Strikes a solitary sound.
Vainly glitter hill and plain,
And the air is calm in vain;
Vainly Morning spreads the lure

Of a sky serene and pure;
Creature none can she decoy
Into open sign of joy:
Is it that they have a fear
Of the dreary season near?
Or that other pleasures be
Sweeter even than gaiety?
Yet, whate'er enjoyments dwell
In the impenetrable cell
Of the silent heart which Nature
Furnishes to every creature;
Whatsoe'er we feel and know
Too sedate for outward show, 0
Such a light of gladness breaks,
Pretty Kitten! from thy freaks, —
Spreads with such a living grace
O'er my little Dora's face;
Yes, the sight so stirs and charms
Thee, Baby, laughing in my arms,
That almost I could repine
That your transports are not mine,
That I do not wholly fare
Even as ye do, thoughtless pair!
And I will have my careless season
Spite of melancholy reason,
Will walk through life in such a way
That, when time brings on decay,
Now and then I may possess
Hours of perfect gladsomeness.
 —Pleased by any random toy;
By a kitten's busy joy,
Or an infant's laughing eye
Sharing in the ecstasy;

I would fare like that or this,
Find my wisdom in my bliss;
Keep the sprightly soul awake,
And have faculties to take,
Even from things by sorrow wrought,
Matter for a jocund thought,
Spite of care, and spite of grief,
To gambol with Life's falling Leaf.

04. Lucy Gray

Oft had I heard of Lucy Gray,
And when I crossed the Wild,
I chanced to see at break of day
The solitary Child.

No Mate, no comrade Lucy knew;
She dwelt on a wide Moor,
The sweetest Thing that ever grew
Beside a human door!

You yet may spy the Fawn at play,
The Hare upon the Green;
But the sweet face of Lucy Gray
Will never more be seen.

'To-night will be a stormy night,
You to the Town must go,
And take a lantern, Child, to light
Your Mother thro' the snow.'

'That, Father! will I gladly do;
'Tis scarcely afternoon —

The Minster-clock has just struck two,
And yonder is the Moon.'

At this the Father raised his hook
And snapped a faggot-band;
He plied his work, and Lucy took
The lantern in her hand.

Not blither is the mountain roe,
With many a wanton stroke
Her feet disperse the powd'ry snow
That rises up like smoke.

The storm came on before its time,
She wandered up and down,
And many a hill did Lucy climb
But never reached the Town.

The wretched Parents all that night
Went shouting far and wide;
But there was neither sound nor sight
To serve them for a guide.

At day-break on a hill they stood
That overlooked the Moor;
And thence they saw the Bridge of Wood
A furlong from their door.

And now they homeward turned, and cried
'In Heaven we all shall meet!'
When in the snow the Mother spied
The print of Lucy's feet.

Then downward from the steep hill's edge
They tracked the footmarks small;
And through the broken hawthorn-hedge,
And by the long stone-wall;

And then an open field they crossed,
The marks were still the same;
They tracked them on, nor ever lost,
And to the Bridge they came.

They followed from the snowy bank
The footmarks, one by one,
Into the middle of the plank,
And further there were none.

Yet some maintain that to this day
She is a living Child,
That you may see sweet Lucy Gray
Upon the lonesome Wild.

O'er rough and smooth she trips along,
And never looks behind;
And sings a solitary song
That whistles in the wind.

05. Expostulation and Reply (1798)

"Expostulation" means protest or complaint.

"Why, William, on that old grey stone,
Thus for the length of half a day,
Why, William, sit you thus alone,
And dream your time away?

"Where are your books? —that light bequeathed
To Beings else forlorn and blind!
Up! up! and drink the spirit breathed
From dead men to their kind.

"You look round on your Mother Earth,
As if she for no purpose bore you;
As if you were her first-born birth,
And none had lived before you!"

One morning thus, by Esthwaite lake,
When life was sweet, I knew not why,
To me my good friend Matthew spake,
And thus I made reply:

"The eye —it cannot choose but see;
We cannot bid the ear be still;
Our bodies feel, where'er they be,
Against or with our will.

"Nor less I deem that there are Powers
Which of themselves our minds impress;
That we can feed this mind of ours
In a wise passiveness.

"Think you, 'mid all this mighty sum
Of things for ever speaking,
That nothing of itself will come,
But we must still be seeking?

" —Then ask not wherefore, here, alone,
Conversing as I may,

I sit upon this old grey stone,
And dream my time away."

06. The Tables Turned (An Evening Scene on the Same Subject)

Up! up! my Friend, and quit your books;
Or surely you'll grow double:
Up! up! my Friend, and clear your looks;
Why all this toil and trouble?

The sun, above the mountain's head,
A freshening lustre mellow
Through all the long green fields has spread,
His first sweet evening yellow.

Books! 'tis a dull and endless strife:
Come, hear the woodland linnet,
How sweet his music! on my life,
There's more of wisdom in it.

And hark! how blithe the throstle sings!
He, too, is no mean preacher:
Come forth into the light of things,
Let Nature be your teacher.

She has a world of ready wealth,
Our minds and hearts to bless —
Spontaneous wisdom breathed by health,
Truth breathed by cheerfulness.

One impulse from a vernal wood
May teach you more of man,

Of moral evil and of good,
Than all the sages can.

Sweet is the lore which Nature brings;
Our meddling intellect
Mis-shapes the beauteous forms of things —
We murder to dissect.

Enough of Science and of Art;
Close up those barren leaves;
Come forth, and bring with you a heart
That watches and receives.

07. She Dwelt Among the Untrodden Ways

She dwelt among the untrodden ways
Beside the springs of Dove,
A Maid whom there were none to praise
And very few to love:

A violet by a mossy stone
Half hidden from the eye!
—Fair as a star, when only one
Is shining in the sky.

She lived unknown, and few could know
When Lucy ceased to be;
But she is in her grave, and, oh,
The difference to me!

08. To a Child Written in Her Album

Small service is true service while it lasts:
Of humblest Friends, bright Creature! scorn not one:

The Daisy, by the shadow that it casts,
Protects the lingering dew-drop from the Sun.

09. I Travelled Among Unknown Men

I travelled among unknown men,
In lands beyond the sea;
Nor, England! did I know till then
What love I bore to thee.

'Tis past, that melancholy dream!
Nor will I quit thy shore
A second time; for still I seem
To love thee more and more.

Among thy mountains did I feel
The joy of my desire;
And she I cherished turned her wheel
Beside an English fire.

Thy mornings showed, thy nights concealed
The bowers where Lucy played;
And thine too is the last green field
That Lucy's eyes surveyed.

10. She Was a Phantom of Delight

Wordsworth included this note: "Written at Town-end, Grasmere. The germ of this poem was four lines composed as a part of the verses on the Highland Girl. Though beginning in this way, it was written from my heart, as is sufficiently obvious."

She was a Phantom of delight
When first she gleamed upon my sight;
A lovely Apparition, sent
To be a moment's ornament;
Her eyes as stars of Twilight fair;
Like Twilight's, too, her dusky hair;
But all things else about her drawn
From May-time and the cheerful Dawn;
A dancing Shape, an Image gay,
To haunt, to startle, and way-lay.

I saw her upon nearer view,
A Spirit, yet a Woman too!
Her household motions light and free,
And steps of virgin-liberty;
A countenance in which did meet
Sweet records, promises as sweet;
A Creature not too bright or good
For human nature's daily food;
For transient sorrows, simple wiles,
Praise, blame, love, kisses, tears, and smiles.

And now I see with eye serene
The very pulse of the machine;
A Being breathing thoughtful breath,
A Traveller between life and death;

The reason firm, the temperate will,
Endurance, foresight, strength, and skill;
A perfect Woman, nobly planned,
To warn, to comfort, and command;
And yet a Spirit still, and bright
With something of angelic light.

11. The Rainbow

My heart leaps up when I behold
    A rainbow in the sky:
So was it when my life began;
So is it now I am a man;
So be it when I shall grow old,
    Or let me die!
The Child is father of the Man;
I could wish my days to be
Bound each to each by natural piety.

12. To the Cuckoo

O Blithe New-comer! I have heard,
I hear thee and rejoice.
O Cuckoo! shall I call thee Bird,
Or but a wandering Voice?

While I am lying on the grass
Thy twofold shout I hear,
From hill to hill it seems to pass,
At once far off, and near.

Though babbling only to the Vale,
Of sunshine and of flowers,

Thou bringest unto me a tale
Of visionary hours.

Thrice welcome, darling of the Spring!
Even yet thou art to me
No bird, but an invisible thing,
A voice, a mystery;

The same whom in my school-boy days
I listened to; that Cry
Which made me look a thousand ways
In bush, and tree, and sky.

To seek thee did I often rove
Through woods and on the green;
And thou wert still a hope, a love;
Still longed for, never seen.

And I can listen to thee yet;
Can lie upon the plain
And listen, till I do beget
That golden time again.

O blessed Bird! the earth we pace
Again appears to be
An unsubstantial, faery place;
That is fit home for Thee!

13. The Green Linnet

A green linnet is a bird, also called a greenfinch.

Beneath these fruit-tree boughs that shed
Their snow-white blossoms on my head,

Wordsworth

With brightest sunshine round me spread
Of spring's unclouded weather,
In this sequestered nook how sweet
To sit upon my orchard-seat!
And birds and flowers once more to greet,
My last year's friends together.

One have I marked, the happiest guest
In all this covert of the blest:
Hail to Thee, far above the rest
In joy of voice and pinion!
Thou, Linnet! in thy green array,
Presiding Spirit here to-day,
Dost lead the revels of the May;
And this is thy dominion.

While birds, and butterflies, and flowers,
Make all one band of paramours,
Thou, ranging up and down the bowers,
Art sole in thy employment:
A Life, a Presence like the Air,
Scattering thy gladness without care,
Too blest with any one to pair;
Thyself thy own enjoyment.

Amid yon tuft of hazel trees,
That twinkle to the gusty breeze,
Behold him perched in ecstasies,
Yet seeming still to hover;
There! where the flutter of his wings
Upon his back and body flings
Shadows and sunny glimmerings,
That cover him all over.

My dazzled sight he oft deceives,
A Brother of the dancing leaves;
Then flits, and from the cottage-eaves
Pours forth his song in gushes;
As if by that exulting strain
He mocked and treated with disdain
The voiceless Form he chose to feign,
While fluttering in the bushes.

14. To the Small Celandine (Common Pilewort)

Wordsworth added this note: "It is remarkable that this flower, coming out so early in the spring as it does, and so bright and beautiful, and in such profusion, should not have been noticed earlier in English verse. What adds much to the interest that attends it is its habit of shutting itself up and opening out according to the degree of light and temperature of the air." Celandine grew in the garden at Dove Cottage, which was largely cultivated and arranged by his sister Dorothy. She said that the celandine was William's favorite flower.

Pansies, lilies, kingcups, daisies,
Let them live upon their praises;
Long as there's a sun that sets,
Primroses will have their glory;
Long as there are violets,
They will have a place in story:
There's a flower that shall be mine,
'Tis the little Celandine.

Eyes of some men travel far
For the finding of a star;

Wordsworth

Up and down the heavens they go,
Men that keep a mighty rout!
I'm as great as they, I trow,
Since the day I found thee out,
Little Flower! —I'll make a stir,
Like a sage astronomer.

Modest, yet withal an Elf
Bold, and lavish of thyself;
Since we needs must first have met
I have seen thee, high and low,
Thirty years or more, and yet
'Twas a face I did not know;
Thou hast now, go where I may,
Fifty greetings in a day.

Ere a leaf is on a bush,
In the time before the thrush
Has a thought about her nest,
Thou wilt come with half a call,
Spreading out thy glossy breast
Like a careless Prodigal;
Telling tales about the sun,
When we've little warmth, or none.

Poets, vain men in their mood!
Travel with the multitude:
Never heed them; I aver
That they all are wanton wooers;
But the thrifty cottager,
Who stirs little out of doors,
Joys to spy thee near her home;
Spring is coming, Thou art come!

Comfort have thou of thy merit,
Kindly, unassuming Spirit!
Careless of thy neighbourhood,
Thou dost show thy pleasant face
On the moor, and in the wood,
In the lane; —there's not a place,
Howsoever mean it be,
But 'tis good enough for thee.

Ill befall the yellow flowers,
Children of the flaring hours!
Buttercups, that will be seen,
Whether we will see or no;
Others, too, of lofty mien;
They have done as worldlings do,
Taken praise that should be thine,
Little, humble Celandine!

Prophet of delight and mirth,
Ill-requited upon earth;
Herald of a mighty band,
Of a joyous train ensuing,
Serving at my heart's command,
Tasks that are no tasks renewing,
I will sing, as doth behove,
Hymns in praise of what I love!

15. To the Same Flower

Pleasures newly found are sweet
When they lie about our feet:

February last, my heart
First at sight of thee was glad;
All unheard of as thou art,
Thou must needs, I think, have had,
Celandine! and long ago,
Praise of which I nothing know.

I have not a doubt but he,
Whosoe'er the man might be,
Who the first with pointed rays
(Workman worthy to be sainted)
Set the sign-board in a blaze,
When the rising sun he painted,
Took the fancy from a glance
At thy glittering countenance.

Soon as gentle breezes bring
News of winter's vanishing,
And the children build their bowers,
Sticking 'kerchief-plots of mould
All about with full-blown flowers,
Thick as sheep in shepherd's fold!
With the proudest thou art there,
Mantling in the tiny square.

Often have I sighed to measure
By myself a lonely pleasure,
Sighed to think, I read a book
Only read, perhaps, by me;
Yet I long could overlook
Thy bright coronet and Thee,
And thy arch and wily ways,
And thy store of other praise.

Blithe of heart, from week to week
Thou dost play at hide-and-seek;
While the patient primrose sits
Like a beggar in the cold,
Thou, a flower of wiser wits,
Slipp'st into thy sheltering hold;
Liveliest of the vernal train
When ye all are out again.

Drawn by what peculiar spell,
By what charm of sight or smell,
Does the dim-eyed curious Bee,
Labouring for her waxen cells,
Fondly settle upon Thee
Prized above all buds and bells
Opening daily at thy side,
By the season multiplied?

Thou art not beyond the moon,
But a thing "beneath our shoon";
Let the bold Discoverer thrid
In his bark the polar sea;
Rear who will a pyramid;
Praise it is enough for me,
If there be but three or four
Who will love my little Flower.

16. To the Daisy

Wordsworth said that some of his readers complained about his use of the phrase "thy function apostolical" as applied to the lowly daisy. "Apostolical" meant having something to do particularly with the Twelve Apostles, or it could refer more generally to the leaders of the Christian church. Wordsworth pointed out that nothing could be more appropriate, since the original Apostles were "sent on a mission," and that "this little flower...may be regarded, in its humble degree, as administering both to moral and to spiritual purposes."

Bright Flower! whose home is everywhere,
Bold in maternal Nature's care,
And all the long year through the heir
      Of joy or sorrow;
Methinks that there abides in thee
Some concord with humanity,
Given to no other flower I see
      The forest thorough!

Is it that Man is soon deprest?
A thoughtless Thing! who, once unblest,
Does little on his memory rest,
      Or on his reason,
And Thou would'st teach him how to find
A shelter under every wind,
A hope for times that are unkind
      And every season?

Thou wander'st the wide world about,
Unchecked by pride or scrupulous doubt,
With friends to greet thee, or without,
      Yet pleased and willing;
Meek, yielding to the occasion's call,
And all things suffering from all
Thy function apostolical
      In peace fulfilling.

17. To the Same Flower

With little here to do or see
Of things that in the great world be,
Sweet Daisy! again I talk to thee,
    For thou art worthy,
Thou unassuming Common-place
Of Nature, with that homely face,
And yet with something of a grace,
    Which Love makes for thee!

Oft on the dappled turf at ease
I sit, and play with similies,
Loose types of things through all degrees,
    Thoughts of thy raising:
And many a fond and idle name
I give to thee, for praise or blame,
As is the humour of the game,
    While I am gazing.

A nun demure of lowly port;
Or sprightly maiden, of Love's court,
In thy simplicity the sport
    Of all temptations;
A queen in crown of rubies drest;
A starveling in a scanty vest;
Are all, as seems to suit thee best,
    Thy appellations.

A little cyclops, with one eye
Staring to threaten and defy,
That thought comes next —and instantly
    The freak is over,

The shape will vanish —and behold
A silver shield with boss of gold,
That spreads itself, some faery bold
    In fight to cover!

I see thee glittering from afar —
And then thou art a pretty star;
Not quite so fair as many are
    In heaven above thee!
Yet like a star, with glittering crest,
Self-poised in air thou seem'st to rest; —
May peace come never to his nest,
    Who shall reprove thee!

Bright 'Flower'! for by that name at last,
When all my reveries are past,
I call thee, and to that cleave fast,
    Sweet silent creature!
That breath'st with me in sun and air,
Do thou, as thou art wont, repair
My heart with gladness, and a share
    Of thy meek nature!

18. The World is Too Much with Us; Late and Soon

In Greek mythology, Proteus was the shepherd of the sea's flocks (or seals). Triton was the son of the sea god, Poseidon. Triton was often shown as having a conch shell which he would blow like a trumpet.

The world is too much with us; late and soon,
Getting and spending, we lay waste our powers:
Little we see in Nature that is ours;
We have given our hearts away, a sordid boon!

The Sea that bares her bosom to the moon;
The winds that will be howling at all hours,
And are up-gathered now like sleeping flowers;
For this, for everything, we are out of tune;
It moves us not —Great God! I'd rather be
A Pagan suckled in a creed outworn;
So might I, standing on this pleasant lea,
Have glimpses that would make me less forlorn;
Have sight of Proteus rising from the sea;
Or hear old Triton blow his wreathed horn.

19. The Redbreast Chasing the Butterfly

Wordsworth noted that he saw the robin and the butterfly in "the beautiful orchard" at Town-end. Now spelled Town End, this is a hamlet (or small village) near the village of Grasmere, near Ambleside. He also added a footnote explaining that "Father Adam" refers to Milton's Paradise Lost, Book XI, *where Adam points out examples of animals and birds pursuing each other.*

Art thou the bird whom Man loves best,
The pious bird with the scarlet breast,
    Our little English Robin;
The bird that comes about our doors
When Autumn-winds are sobbing?
Art thou the Peter of Norway Boors?
    Their Thomas in Finland,
    And Russia far inland?
The bird, that by some name or other
All men who know thee call their brother,
The darling of children and men?
Could Father Adam open his eyes
And see this sight beneath the skies,
He'd wish to close them again.

If the Butterfly knew but his friend,
Hither his flight he would bend;
And find his way to me,
Under the branches of the tree:
In and out, he darts about;
Can this be the bird, to man so good,
That, after their bewildering,
Covered with leaves the little children,
    So painfully in the wood?
What ailed thee, Robin, that thou could'st pursue
    A beautiful creature,
That is gentle by nature?
Beneath the summer sky
From flower to flower let him fly;
'Tis all that he wishes to do.
The cheerer Thou of our in-door sadness,
He is the friend of our summer gladness:
What hinders, then, that ye should be
Playmates in the sunny weather,
And fly about in the air together!
His beautiful wings in crimson are drest,
A crimson as bright as thine own:
Would'st thou be happy in thy nest,
O pious Bird! whom man loves best,
Love him, or leave him alone!

20. Daffodils

Wordsworth noted that "the Daffodils grew and still grow on the margin of Ullswater and probably may be seen to this day as beautiful in the month of March, nodding their golden heads beside the dancing and foaming waves."

I wandered lonely as a cloud
That floats on high o'er vales and hills,
When all at once I saw a crowd,
A host, of golden daffodils;
Beside the lake, beneath the trees,
Fluttering and dancing in the breeze.

Continuous as the stars that shine
And twinkle on the milky way,
They stretched in never-ending line
Along the margin of a bay:
Ten thousand saw I at a glance,
Tossing their heads in sprightly dance.

The waves beside them danced; but they
Out-did the sparkling waves in glee:
A poet could not but be gay,
In such a jocund company:
I gazed–and gazed–but little thought
What wealth the show to me had brought:
For oft, when on my couch I lie
In vacant or in pensive mood,
They flash upon that inward eye
Which is the bliss of solitude;
And then my heart with pleasure fills,
And dances with the daffodils.

21. Personal Talk

Wordsworth wrote this poem while thinking about how much he enjoyed simple, quiet pleasures such as "the loved presence of my cottage-fire," listening to "the flapping of the flame." He also pointed out that "Dreams, books, are each a world; and books, we know, / Are a substantial world." When he published the poem, he included a funny story about the "good old days" when he lived with his sister in Dove Cottage. "My Sister and I were in the habit of having the tea-kettle in our little sitting-room; and we toasted the bread ourselves, which reminds me of a little circumstance not unworthy of being set down among these minutiae. Happening both of us to be engaged a few minutes one morning when we had a young prig of a Scotch lawyer to breakfast with us, my dear Sister, with her usual simplicity, put the toasting-fork with a slice of bread into the hands of this Edinburgh genius. Our little book-case stood on one side of the fire. To prevent loss of time, he took down a book, and fell to reading, to the neglect of the toast, which was burnt to a cinder. Many a time have we laughed at this circumstance, and other cottage simplicities of that day."

I

I am not One who much or oft delight
To season my fireside with personal talk. —
Of friends, who live within an easy walk,
Or neighbours, daily, weekly, in my sight:
And, for my chance-acquaintance, ladies bright,
Sons, mothers, maidens withering on the stalk,
These all wear out of me, like Forms, with chalk
Painted on rich men's floors, for one feast-night.
Better than such discourse doth silence long,
Long, barren silence, square with my desire;
To sit without emotion, hope, or aim,
In the loved presence of my cottage-fire,
And listen to the flapping of the flame,
Or kettle whispering its faint undersong.

II

"Yet life," you say, "is life; we have seen and see,
And with a living pleasure we describe;
And fits of sprightly malice do but bribe
The languid mind into activity.
Sound sense, and love itself, and mirth and glee
Are fostered by the comment and the gibe."
Even be it so; yet still among your tribe,
Our daily world's true Worldlings, rank not me!
Children are blest, and powerful; their world lies
More justly balanced; partly at their feet,
And part far from them: sweetest melodies
Are those that are by distance made more sweet;
Whose mind is but the mind of his own eyes,
He is a Slave; the meanest we can meet!

III

Wings have we, —and as far as we can go,
We may find pleasure: wilderness and wood,
Blank ocean and mere sky, support that mood
Which with the lofty sanctifies the low.
Dreams, books, are each a world; and books, we know,
Are a substantial world, both pure and good:
Round these, with tendrils strong as flesh and blood,
Our pastime and our happiness will grow.
There find I personal themes, a plenteous store,
Matter wherein right voluble I am,
To which I listen with a ready ear;
Two shall be named, pre-eminently dear, —
The gentle Lady married to the Moor;
And heavenly Una with her milk-white Lamb,

IV

Nor can I not believe but that hereby
Great gains are mine; for thus I live remote
From evil-speaking; rancour, never sought,
Comes to me not; malignant truth, or lie.
Hence have I genial seasons, hence have I
Smooth passions, smooth discourse, and joyous thought:
And thus from day to day my little boat
Rocks in its harbour, lodging peaceably.
Blessings be with them—and eternal praise,
Who gave us nobler loves, and nobler cares—
The Poets, who on earth have made us heirs
Of truth and pure delight by heavenly lays!
Oh! might my name be numbered among theirs,
Then gladly would I end my mortal days.

22. Ode to Duty

Wordsworth had read a poem by Thomas Gray called "Ode to Adversity," which showed "Adversity" as if she were a person (it begins "Daughter of Jove, relentless Power, / Thou Tamer of the human breast"). He decided to use a similar pattern to write his own poem about "Duty," a sort of apology to her for his tendency to seek out "smoother walks," taking the easier path instead of doing what was right. He added this thought to his poem: "We should be rigorous to ourselves and forbearing, if not indulgent, to others, and, if we make comparisons at all, it ought to be with those who have morally excelled us."

Stern Daughter of the Voice of God!
O Duty! if that name thou love
Who art a light to guide, a rod
To check the erring, and reprove;
Thou, who art victory and law

When empty terrors overawe;
From vain temptations dost set free;
And calm'st the weary strife of frail humanity!

There are who ask not if thine eye
Be on them; who, in love and truth,
Where no misgiving is, rely
Upon the genial sense of youth:
Glad Hearts! without reproach or blot
Who do thy work, and know it not:
Oh! if through confidence misplaced
They fail, thy saving arms, dread Power! around them cast.

Serene will be our days and bright,
And happy will our nature be,
When love is an unerring light,
And joy its own security.
And they a blissful course may hold
Even now, who, not unwisely bold,
Live in the spirit of this creed;
Yet seek thy firm support, according to their need.

I, loving freedom, and untried;
No sport of every random gust,
Yet being to myself a guide,
Too blindly have reposed my trust:
And oft, when in my heart was heard
Thy timely mandate, I deferred
The task, in smoother walks to stray;
But thee I now would serve more strictly, if I may.

Through no disturbance of my soul,
Or strong compunction in me wrought,

I supplicate for thy control;
But in the quietness of thought:
Me this unchartered freedom tires;
I feel the weight of chance-desires:
My hopes no more must change their name,
I long for a repose that ever is the same.
Stern Lawgiver! yet thou dost wear
The Godhead's most benignant grace;
Nor know we anything so fair
As is the smile upon thy face:
Flowers laugh before thee on their beds
And fragrance in thy footing treads;
Thou dost preserve the stars from wrong;
And the most ancient heavens, through
Thee, are fresh and strong.

To humbler functions, awful Power!
I call thee: I myself commend
Unto thy guidance from this hour;
Oh, let my weakness have an end!
Give unto me, made lowly wise,
The spirit of self-sacrifice;
The confidence of reason give;
And in the light of truth thy Bondman let me live!

23. The Solitary Reaper

Behold her, single in the field,
Yon solitary Highland Lass!
Reaping and singing by herself;
Stop here, or gently pass!
Alone she cuts and binds the grain,

And sings a melancholy strain;
O listen! for the Vale profound
Is overflowing with the sound.

No Nightingale did ever chaunt
More welcome notes to weary bands
Of travellers in some shady haunt,
Among Arabian sands:
A voice so thrilling ne'er was heard
In spring-time from the Cuckoo-bird,
Breaking the silence of the seas
Among the farthest Hebrides.

Will no one tell me what she sings? —
Perhaps the plaintive numbers flow
For old, unhappy, far-off things,
And battles long ago:
Or is it some more humble lay,
Familiar matter of to-day?
Some natural sorrow, loss, or pain,
That has been, and may be again?

Whate'er the theme, the Maiden sang
As if her song could have no ending;
I saw her singing at her work,
And o'er the sickle bending; —
I listened, motionless and still;
And, as I mounted up the hill
The music in my heart I bore,
Long after it was heard no more.

24. To A Sky-Lark (Up with me!")

Up with me! up with me into the clouds!
  For thy song, Lark, is strong;
Up with me, up with me into the clouds!
  Singing, singing,
With clouds and sky about thee ringing,
  Lift me, guide me till I find
That spot which seems so to thy mind!

I have walked through wildernesses dreary
  And to-day my heart is weary;
  Had I now the wings of a Faery,
   Up to thee would I fly.
There is madness about thee, and joy divine
  In that song of thine;
Lift me, guide me high and high
To thy banqueting-place in the sky!
  Joyous as Morning,
  Thou art laughing and scorning;
Thou hast a nest for thy love and thy rest,
And, though little troubled with sloth,
Drunken Lark! thou would'st be loth
To be such a traveller as I.
  Happy, happy Liver,
With a soul as strong as a mountain river
Pouring out praise to the Almighty Giver,
Joy and jollity be with us both!

Alas! my journey, rugged and uneven,
Through prickly moors or dusty ways must wind;
But hearing thee, or others of thy kind,
As full of gladness and as free of heaven,

113

I, with my fate contented, will plod on,
And hope for higher raptures, when Life's day is done.

25. To the Skylark ("Ethereal Minstrel")

Ethereal minstrel! pilgrim of the sky!
Dost thou despise the earth where cares abound?
Or, while the wings aspire, are heart and eye
Both with thy nest upon the dewy ground?
Thy nest which thou canst drop into at will,
Those quivering wings composed, that music still!

Leave to the nightingale her shady wood;
A privacy of glorious light is thine;
Whence thou dost pour upon the world a flood
Of harmony, with instinct more divine;
Type of the wise who soar, but never roam;
True to the kindred points of Heaven and Home!

26. London, 1802

Milton! thou should'st be living at this hour:
England hath need of thee: she is a fen
Of stagnant waters: altar, sword, and pen,
Fireside, the heroic wealth of hall and bower,
Have forfeited their ancient English dower
Of inward happiness. We are selfish men;
Oh! raise us up, return to us again;
And give us manners, virtue, freedom, power.
Thy soul was like a Star, and dwelt apart:
Thou hadst a voice whose sound was like the sea:
Pure as the naked heavens, majestic, free,
So didst thou travel on life's common way,

In cheerful godliness; and yet thy heart
The lowliest duties on herself did lay.

27. Alice Fell, or, Poverty

*One of Wordsworth's friends told him a true story about an event, and asked if he
could write a poem about it. Wordsworth did so, but he said that his critics ridiculed
"the humbleness, meanness if you like, of the subject, together with the homely mode
of treating it," and therefore he left it out of many editions of his* Poems. *Those
who did like it, though, persuaded him that it should be restored to its proper place
in the book.*
    "Duffil" is a kind of woollen cloth used for coats and blankets.

The post-boy drove with fierce career,
For threatening clouds the moon had drowned;
When, as we hurried on, my ear
Was smitten with a startling sound.

As if the wind blew many ways,
I heard the sound, —and more and more;
It seemed to follow with the chaise,
And still I heard it as before.

At length I to the boy called out;
He stopped his horses at the word,
But neither cry, nor voice, nor shout,
Nor aught else like it, could be heard.

The boy then smacked his whip, and fast
The horses scampered through the rain;
But, hearing soon upon the blast
The cry, I bade him halt again.

Forthwith alighting on the ground,
"Whence comes," said I, "this piteous moan?"
And there a little Girl I found,
Sitting behind the chaise, alone.

"My cloak!" no other word she spake,
But loud and bitterly she wept,
As if her innocent heart would break;
And down from off her seat she leapt.

"What ails you, child?" —she sobbed "Look here!"
I saw it in the wheel entangled,
A weather-beaten rag as e'er
From any garden scare-crow dangled.

There, twisted between nave and spoke,
It hung, nor could at once be freed;
But our joint pains unloosed the cloak,
A miserable rag indeed!

"And whither are you going, child,
To-night alone these lonesome ways?"
"To Durham," answered she, half wild —
"Then come with me into the chaise."

Insensible to all relief
Sat the poor girl, and forth did send
Sob after sob, as if her grief
Could never, never have an end.

"My child, in Durham do you dwell?"
She checked herself in her distress,
And said, "My name is Alice Fell;

I'm fatherless and motherless.

"And I to Durham, Sir, belong."
Again, as if the thought would choke
Her very heart, her grief grew strong;
And all was for her tattered cloak!

The chaise drove on; our journey's end
Was nigh; and, sitting by my side,
As if she had lost her only friend
She wept, nor would be pacified.

Up to the tavern-door we post;
Of Alice and her grief I told;
And I gave money to the host,
To buy a new cloak for the old.

"And let it be of duffil grey,
As warm a cloak as man can sell!"
Proud creature was she the next day,
The little orphan, Alice Fell!

28. Characteristics of a Child Three Years Old

A faggot means a bundle of sticks used for fuel.

Loving she is, and tractable, though wild;
And Innocence hath privilege in her
To dignify arch looks and laughing eyes;
And feats of cunning; and the pretty round
Of trespasses, affected to provoke
Mock-chastisement and partnership in play.

And, as a faggot sparkles on the hearth,
Not less if unattended and alone
Than when both young and old sit gathered round
And take delight in its activity;
Even so this happy Creature of herself
Is all-sufficient, solitude to her
Is blithe society, who fills the air
With gladness and involuntary songs.
Light are her sallies as the tripping fawn's
Forth-startled from the fern where she lay couched;
Unthought-of, unexpected, as the stir
Of the soft breeze ruffling the meadow-flowers,
Or from before it chasing wantonly
The many-coloured images imprest
Upon the bosom of a placid lake.

29. To the Supreme Being

Wordsworth wrote this poem as a translation of words written in Italian by the artist Michelangelo.

The prayers I make will then be sweet indeed
If Thou the spirit give by which I pray:
My unassisted heart is barren clay,
That of its native self can nothing feed:
Of good and pious works thou art the seed,
That quickens only where thou say'st it may:
Unless Thou show to us thine own true way
No man can find it: Father! Thou must lead.
Do Thou, then, breathe those thoughts into my mind
By which such virtue may in me be bred
That in thy holy footsteps I may tread;
The fetters of my tongue do Thou unbind,

That I may have the power to sing of thee,
And sound thy praises everlastingly.

30. To a Butterfly ("I've watched you now")

I've watched you now a full half-hour;
Self-poised upon that yellow flower
And, little Butterfly! indeed
I know not if you sleep or feed.
How motionless! —not frozen seas
More motionless! and then
What joy awaits you, when the breeze
Hath found you out among the trees,
And calls you forth again!

This plot of orchard-ground is ours;
My trees they are, my Sister's flowers;
Here rest your wings when they are weary;
Here lodge as in a sanctuary!
Come often to us, fear no wrong;
Sit near us on the bough!
We'll talk of sunshine and of song,
And summer days, when we were young;
Sweet childish days, that were as long
    As twenty days are now.

31. The Reverie of Poor Susan

A reverie is a daydream. Here, a bird's song prompts a memory, which stirs Susan's imagination.

At the corner of Wood Street, when daylight appears,
Hangs a Thrush that sings loud, it has sung for three years:

Poor Susan has passed by the spot, and has heard
In the silence of morning the song of the Bird.

'Tis a note of enchantment; what ails her? She sees
A mountain ascending, a vision of trees;
Bright volumes of vapour through Lothbury glide,
And a river flows on through the vale of Cheapside.

Green pastures she views in the midst of the dale,
Down which she so often has tripped with her pail;
And a single small cottage, a nest like a dove's,
The one only dwelling on earth that she loves.

She looks, and her heart is in heaven: but they fade,
The mist and the river, the hill and the shade:
The stream will not flow, and the hill will not rise,
And the colours have all passed away from her eyes!

32. A Character

*I wonder if Wordsworth had been examining the countenance of anybody in
particular, or if this was a general observation? —W.C.*

I marvel how Nature could ever find space
For so many strange contrasts in one human face:
There's thought and no thought, and there's paleness and bloom
And bustle and sluggishness, pleasure and gloom.

There's weakness, and strength both redundant and vain;
Such strength as, if ever affliction and pain
Could pierce through a temper that's soft to disease,
Would be rational peace —a philosopher's ease.

There's indifference, alike when he fails or succeeds,

And attention full ten times as much as there needs;
Pride where there's no envy, there's so much of joy;
And mildness, and spirit both forward and coy.

There's freedom, and sometimes a diffident stare
Of shame scarcely seeming to know that she's there,
There's virtue, the title it surely may claim,
Yet wants heaven knows what to be worthy the name.

This picture from nature may seem to depart,
Yet the Man would at once run away with your heart;
And I for five centuries right gladly would be
Such an odd such a kind happy creature as he.

33. from Poems Composed or Suggested

During a Tour in the Summer of 1833

*On catching birds with lime —bird lime is a sticky substance spread on branches
of trees for the purpose of catching birds alive. Traditionally made of various
substances, in England it was commonly made by boiling holly. It's illegal in most
places today.*

III

They called Thee MERRY ENGLAND, in old time;
A happy people won for thee that name
With envy heard in many a distant clime;
And, spite of change, for me thou keep'st the same
Endearing title, a responsive chime
To the heart's fond belief; though some there are
Whose sterner judgments deem that word a snare
For inattentive Fancy, like the lime
Which foolish birds are caught with. Can, I ask,
This face of rural beauty be a mask

For discontent, and poverty, and crime;
These spreading towns a cloak for lawless will?
Forbid it, Heaven! —and MERRY ENGLAND still
Shall be thy rightful name, in prose and rhyme!

34. Thought of a Briton on the Subjugation of Switzerland

Napoleon's troops, having conquered Italy and Prussia previously, attacked Switzerland in February of 1798. He intervened again in 1803, which prompted Wordsworth's outrage.

Two Voices are there; one is of the sea,
One of the mountains; each a mighty Voice:
In both from age to age thou didst rejoice,
They were thy chosen music, Liberty!
There came a Tyrant, and with holy glee
Thou fought'st against him; but hast vainly striven:
Thou from thy Alpine holds at length art driven,
Where not a torrent murmurs heard by thee.
Of one deep bliss thine ear hath been bereft:
Then cleave, O cleave to that which still is left;
For, high-souled Maid, what sorrow would it be
That Mountain floods should thunder as before,
And Ocean bellow from his rocky shore,
And neither awful Voice be heard by thee!

35. To A Butterfly ("Stay near me")

From his sister Dorothy's journal: "Sunday Morning. —William . . . got up at nine o'clock, but before he rose he had finished The Beggar Boy, and while we were at breakfast . . . he wrote the poem To a Butterfly! He ate not a morsel, but sate with his shirt neck unbuttoned, and his waistcoat open while he did it. The thought first came upon him as we were talking about the pleasure we both always felt at the sight of a butterfly. I told him that I used to chase them a little, but that I was afraid of brushing the dust off their wings, and did not catch them. He told me how he used to kill all the white ones when he went to school because they were Frenchmen . . . I wrote it down and the other poems, and I read them all over to him . . . William began to try to alter The Butterfly, and tired himself . . ."

Stay near me —do not take thy flight!
A little longer stay in sight!
Much converse do I find in thee,
Historian of my infancy!
Float near me; do not yet depart!
Dead times revive in thee:
Thou bring'st, gay creature as thou art!
A solemn image to my heart,
My father's family!

Oh! pleasant, pleasant were the days,
The time, when, in our childish plays,
My sister Emmeline and I
Together chased the butterfly!
A very hunter did I rush
Upon the prey: —with leaps and springs
I followed on from brake to bush;
But she, God love her, feared to brush
The dust from off its wings.

36. To H. C. Six Years Old

H.C. is Hartley Coleridge, the son of the Wordsworth's dear friend Samuel Taylor Coleridge and his wife. William and Dorothy kept him for a few weeks when his mother was pregnant with his younger sibling, and he lived with them again for a time while he attended the local school.

O thou! whose fancies from afar are brought;
Who of thy words dost make a mock apparel,
And fittest to unutterable thought

123

The breeze-like motion and the self-born carol;
Thou faery voyager! that dost float
In such clear water, that thy boat
May rather seem
To brood on air than on an earthly stream;
Suspended in a stream as clear as sky,
Where earth and heaven do make one imagery;
O blessed vision! happy child!
Thou art so exquisitely wild,
I think of thee with many fears
For what may be thy lot in future years.

    I thought of times when Pain might be thy guest,
Lord of thy house and hospitality;
And Grief, uneasy lover! never rest
But when she sate within the touch of thee.
O too industrious folly!
O vain and causeless melancholy!
Nature will either end thee quite;
Or, lengthening out thy season of delight,
Preserve for thee, by individual right,
A young lamb's heart among the full-grown flocks.
What hast thou to do with sorrow,
Or the injuries of to-morrow?
Thou art a dew-drop, which the morn brings forth,
Ill fitted to sustain unkindly shocks,
Or to be trailed along the soiling earth;
A gem that glitters while it lives,
And no forewarning gives;
But, at the touch of wrong, without a strife
Slips in a moment out of life.

37. Written in Very Early Youth

"Kine" is an old fashioned word for cows, popularly used in poetry and crossword puzzles. "Officious" is meddling, doing favors or offering advice and help that one neither wants nor needs.

Calm is all nature as a resting wheel.
The kine are couched upon the dewy grass;
The horse alone, seen dimly as I pass,
Is cropping audibly his later meal:
Dark is the ground; a slumber seems to steal
O'er vale, and mountain, and the starless sky.
Now, in this blank of things, a harmony,
Home-felt, and home-created, comes to heal
That grief for which the senses still supply
Fresh food; for only then, when memory
Is hushed, am I at rest. My Friends! restrain
Those busy cares that would allay my pain;
Oh! leave me to myself, nor let me feel
The officious touch that makes me droop again.

38. Written While Sailing in a Boat at Evening

Wordsworth said that this poem wasn't really composed in a boat at all. He was taking a solitary walk on the banks of the River Cam in Cambridge when he was struck by the appearance of the scene. When he published the poem he moved the river to the Thames, and the poet's location to a boat.

How richly glows the water's breast
Before us, tinged with evening hues,
While, facing thus the crimson west,
The boat her silent course pursues!

And see how dark the backward stream!
A little moment past so smiling!
And still, perhaps, with faithless gleam,
Some other loiterers beguiling.

Such views the youthful Bard allure;
But, heedless of the following gloom,
He deems their colours shall endure
Till peace go with him to the tomb.
　—And let him nurse his fond deceit,
And what if he must die in sorrow!
Who would not cherish dreams so sweet,
Though grief and pain may come to-morrow?

39. The Eagle and the Dove

This is a translation Wordsworth made of a French poem. Caractacus was a British chieftain who staunchly resisted the Romans for several years.

Shade of Caractacus, if spirits love
The cause they fought for in their earthly home
To see the Eagle ruffled by the Dove
May soothe thy memory of the chains of Rome.

These children claim thee for their sire; the breath
Of thy renown, from Cambrian mountains, fans
A flame within them that despises death
And glorifies the truant youth of Vannes.

With thy own scorn of tyrants they advance,
But truth divine has sanctified their rage,
A silver cross enchased with flowers of France
Their badge, attests the holy fight they wage.

The shrill defiance of the young crusade
Their veteran foes mock as an idle noise;
But unto Faith and Loyalty comes aid
From Heaven, gigantic force to beardless boys.

40. Ode

This is part of a 206-line poem titled Ode: Intimations of Immortality from Recollections of Early Childhood. An ode is a formal lyric poem that is written in celebration or dedication of something beautiful or worth celebrating.

While Earth herself is adorning
This sweet May morning,
And the children are culling on every side
In a thousand valleys far and wide,
Fresh flowers; while the sun shines warm
And the Babe leaps up on its mother's arm —

Then sing ye Birds, sing, sing a joyous song
And let the young lambs bound as to the tabor's sound
We in thought will join your throng
Ye that pipe and ye that play
Ye that through your hearts today
Feel the gladness of the May.

A suggested extra poem for those who enjoy Wordsworth:
Lines Written a Few Miles Above Tintern Abbey (also called *Tintern Abbey*).

About AmblesideOnline

This book is one in a series of six, each volume corresponding to the poetry suggestions for Years 1-6 in the AmblesideOnline curriculum.

AmblesideOnline's free Charlotte Mason homeschool curriculum prepares children for a life of rich relationships with God, humanity, and the natural world. Named for the area surrounding Charlotte Mason's schools in England, the AmblesideOnline curriculum is the product of a continuing effort towards a specific vision: to design a course of study that would provide as close a modern approximation as possible of the curriculum created by Charlotte Mason for her PNEU Schools, within the limitations of the current availability of books and materials that match Mason's high standards.

The Advisory, with the assistance of the Auxiliary, lead this work.

The contents of this poetry series, as well as our entire twelve-year curriculum and many other resources, are also available on our website.

amblesideonline.org

Printed in Great Britain
by Amazon